Psychoanalysis and the Future of Theory

B

THE BUCKNELL LECTURES IN LITERARY THEORY
General Editors: Michael Payne and Harold Schweizer

The lectures in this series explore some of the fundamental changes in literary studies that have occurred during the past thirty years in response to new work in feminism, Marxism, psychoanalysis, and deconstruction. They assess the impact of these changes and examine specific texts in the light of this new work. Each volume in the series includes a critical assessment of the lecturer's own publications, an interview, and a comprehensive bibliography.

Forthcoming volumes by Peter Brooks, Barbara Johnson, and Stanley Cavell.

Psychoanalysis and the Future of Theory

Malcolm Bowie

BLACKWELL
Oxford UK & Cambridge USA

Copyright © Malcolm Bowie 1993

The right of Malcolm Bowie to be identified as author of this work has been asserted in accordance with the Copyright, Designs and Patents Act 1988.

First published 1993

First published in USA 1994

Blackwell Publishers
108 Cowley Road
Oxford OX4 1JF
UK

238 Main Street
Cambridge, Massachusetts 02142
USA

British Library Cataloguing in Publication Data

A CIP catalogue record for this book is available from the British Library.

Library of Congress Cataloging-in-Publication Data

Bowie, Malcolm.
    Psychoanalysis and the future of theory / Malcolm Bowie.
        p.   cm. — (The Bucknell lectures in literary theory; 9)
    Includes bibliographical references and index.
    ISBN 0–631–18925–4 (alk. paper). — ISBN 0–631–18926–2 (pbk.: alk. paper)
    1. Psychoanalysis. 2. Critical theory. 3. Psychoanalysis and the arts. 4. Freud, Sigmund, 1856–1939. 5. Lacan, Jacques.
I. Title. II. Series.
    BF175.B635   1994
    150.19'5—dc20   93–25937
                                                               CIP

Typeset in 11 on 13 pt Plantin
by Pure Tech Corporation, Pondicherry, India
Printed in Great Britain by Biddles Ltd, Guildford, Surrey
This book is printed on acid-free paper

. . . we will not anticipate the past; – so mind young people – our retrospection will now be all to the future.

Mrs Malaprop in Sheridan's *The Rivals*

Contents

Preface

Fundamental and far-reaching changes in literary studies, often compared to paradigmatic shifts in the sciences, have been taking place during the last thirty years. These changes have included enlarging the literary canon not only to include novels, poems, and plays by writers whose race, gender, or nationality had marginalized their work, but also to include texts by philosophers, psychoanalysts, historians, anthropologists, and social and religious thinkers, who previously were studied by critics merely as 'background'. The stance of the critic and student of literature is also now more in question than ever before. In 1951 it was possible for Cleanth Brooks to declare with confidence that the critic's job was to describe and evaluate literary objects, implying the relevance for criticism of the model of scientific objectivity, while leaving unasked questions concerning significant issues in scientific theory, such as complementarity, indeterminacy, and the use of metaphor. Now the possibility of value-free scepticism is itself in doubt as many feminist, Marxist, and psychoanalytic theorists have stressed the inescapability of ideology and the consequent obligation of teachers and students of literature to declare their political, axiological, and aesthetic positions in order to make those positions conscious and available for examination. Such expansion and deepening of literary studies has, for many critics, revitalized their field.

Those for whom the theoretical revolution has been regenerative would readily echo, and apply to criticism, Lacan's call to revitalize psychoanalysis: 'I consider it to be an urgent task to disengage from concepts that are being deadened by routine use the meaning that they regain both from a re-examination of their history and from a reflexion on their subjective foundations. That, no doubt, is the teacher's prime function.'

Many practising writers and teachers of literature, however, see recent developments in literary theory as dangerous and anti-humanistic. They would insist that displacement of the centrality of the word, claims for the 'death of the author', emphasis upon gaps and incapacities in language, and indiscriminate opening of the canon threaten to marginalize literature itself. On this view the advance of theory is possible only because of literature's retreat in the face of aggressive moves by Marxism, feminism, deconstruction, and psychoanalysis. Furthermore, at a time of militant conservatism and the dominance of corporate values in America and Western Europe, literary theory threatens to diminish further the declining audience for literature and criticism. Theoretical books are difficult to read; they usually assume that their readers possess knowledge that few who have received a traditional literary education have; they often require massive reassessments of language, meaning, and the world; they seem to draw their life from suspect branches of other disciplines: professional philosophers usually avoid Derrida; psychoanalysts dismiss Freud as unscientific; Lacan was excommunicated even by the International Psycho-Analytical Association.

The volumes in this series record part of the attempt at Bucknell University to sustain conversation about changes in literary studies, the impact of those changes on literary art, and the significance of literary theory for the humanities and human sciences. A generous grant from the Andrew W. Mellon Foundation has made possible a five-year series of visiting lectureships by internationally known participants in the reshaping of literary studies. Each volume includes a comprehensive introduction to the published work of the lecturer, the Bucknell Lectures, an interview, and a comprehensive bibliography.

ACKNOWLEDGEMENTS

For permission to reprint material that has already appeared elsewhere, I am grateful to the editors of *Raritan* and *Comparative Criticism*; and to Polity Press and the editors of *Modernism and the European Unconscious*. Tiepolo's *The Finding of Moses* is reproduced by permission of the National Galleries of Scotland, and the drawings accompanying Freud's essay on Michelangelo's *Moses* by permission of Hogarth Press and the Insitute of Psycho-Analysis. My special thanks go to Michael Payne for his hospitality during my visit to Bucknell University and for his support and advice at all stages since; and to Sally Roberts, Duncan Large, Andrew McNeillie, and Jean van Altena for the care and good sense with which they have prepared the text of my lectures for publication.

MB

Introduction

In his recent Modern Masters volume, *Lacan*, Malcolm Bowie expresses his delight in Lacan's promotion of the future perfect as the tense that best captures in language the temporality of the human subject:

> The future perfect . . . emerges as the tense *par excellence* of desire and the prospective human imagination. It allows us to envisage as already complete what has not yet been fully launched, and places us already beyond the goal that we have yet to reach. Desire-in-pursuit and the subject in process have been relocated at precise points of articulation within the signifying chain. (185)

This passage conveniently gathers together several of the topics that Professor Bowie has explored in his four earlier books: In *Henri Michaux: A Study of his Literary Works* (1973), Bowie writes about a poet who not only envisions the human personality without a fixed or stable identity, but who also achieves a new kind of stability in the face of human multiplicity and difficulty. Although *Mallarmé and the Art of being Difficult* (1978) begins with the argument that poetry may be at once pleasurable and difficult, it concludes with a warning against bringing 'chaste' critical assumptions to works of art. Bowie demonstrates that Mallarmé's 'Prose pour des Esseintes' and *Un Coup de dés* defy the defensive and complacent formalist presuppositions that works of art are 'self-bounded worlds in which all tensions are internally resolved and all pains internally soothed and that the personality of their creator (if he has a personality) is irrelevant to them' (154). *Freud, Proust, and Lacan: Theory as Fiction* (1987) further intensifies the arguments for considering and affirming the destabilized subject and work of art by assaulting the definitional boundaries of theory (and truth) and fiction (and imagination). Here Bowie argues that Freud, Proust, and Lacan, 'while having a powerful urge towards Truth, [are] prepared to suspend that urge for indefinite periods during which the mere verbalised wishes of the self and others are lingeringly sketched and compared – as if the truth-seeker who dwelt knowingly among fictions were indeed already at his journey's end' (7). In his elegant monograph on Lacan (1991), Bowie shows that Lacan cultivates purposefully difficult, hybrid, unstable, eroticized texts in order both to expose ingrained falsehood in the ego and to develop an imaginative theory that manifests human desire, which it longs for but dare not (and cannot) grasp.

It is tempting to read these four books as obsessively preoccupied with a single theme – the difficult manifestations of human desire in artistic and theoretical works of imagination – and to see that theme replayed with variations supplied by Michaux, Mallarmé, Freud, Proust, and Lacan. Indeed, desire perpetually in pursuit of its ends is Bowie's recurring concern; but this inescapable topic manifests itself in richly elaborated and various ways. In each of the four books the theoretical threshold is differently placed. The books on Michaux and Mallarmé are studies in literary criticism that proceed through sequences of carefully orchestrated textual explication. The 'Concluding Note' to the Mallarmé book, however, is clearly marked off from the rest of the text by this quotation from *Antony and Cleopatra*:

> . . . fie upon 'But yet'!
> 'But yet' is as a gaoler to bring forth
> Some monstrous malefactor.

This passage ushers in some 'monstrous' theoretical reflections. Mallarmé's poems are difficult in ways that
have 'the power to hurt' (153) beyond the capacity of
any critical act – however conscientious and elegant – to
explain, neutralize, and control. Perplexity and hesitation are legitimately part of the experience of reading
modern poetry, and criticism runs the risk of working
too hard to disguise contradiction and to invent continuity. Here theoretical reflection, which includes the 'but
yet', is a corrective to criticism. In the book on Freud,
Proust, and Lacan, the theoretical threshold is located
in the introduction. Instead of being invited to step
through the back door and outside criticism to reflect on
what it can or cannot do, the reader is here asked
straightaway to consider such questions as 'What are
theorists desiring when they theorise upon desire?' (11).
But no sooner are such questions asked than they are
seductively, though self-effacingly, withdrawn. Whereas
theory might properly address such questions, Bowie
insists that what he offers is merely 'theory-tinged literary
criticism' (11). Nevertheless, Bowie's criticism is animated by its celebration of difficulty and multiplicity, by
its continual recognition of criticism's limitations, and by
its longing to reach beyond itself in order to participate
in the music of art and to share the visions of theory.
Images of movement abound in Bowie's prose: docking
manoeuvres, staging posts, pursuits, flights, anticipated
arrivals, points of departure, arrivals where one has already been, being hunted and hounded, return journeys,
marches, traffic – these are but a few of his tropes for
the ceaseless dynamism of the desiring subject.

There are two sorts of writing that Bowie seems most
to admire. The first is a replaying in language of mute

experience in such a way as to create for the reader as perfect an equivalent of the original experience as language can offer. Lacan's rereading of Freud's account of the 'burning child' dream is an example of this sort. In *The Interpretation of Dreams* Freud gives an account of a father's dream that occurs when he falls asleep during a death-watch in a room adjoining the place where his son's body lies. A candle has fallen over, burning the bedclothes and the dead child's arm. In the dream the child comes to the sleeping father and in a reproachful whisper says, 'Father, don't you see I'm burning?' Freud reads the dream as the replaying of what may have been spoken during the child's terminal fever. Lacan, on the other hand, sees the dream as suspended between two 'reals': 'the sound of the falling candle on the one hand and the phantasmal sound of the son's voice on the other' (105). Here is Bowie's comment on Lacan's interpretation:

> But this dream-voice is remarkable not simply for the physical effect that it produces on the father, who wakes up, but for the fact that it repeats, in its clarity, incisiveness and cruel efficacy the moment of bereavement itself: it is an accident that repeats an accident, an irreducible fragment of the real that speaks of irrecoverable loss, an encounter that is peremptory and brutal and yet one that can now never, outside dreams, take place. Is the real outside or inside? Is it a vacuum or a plenum? Does one chance to meet it, or chance not to meet it? In Lacan's rereading of Freud's celebrated dream-narrative, the undecidability of the concept 'Real' is scrupulously preserved. The Real is an uncrossable threshold for the subject, and not one that can be sidestepped in the analytic encounter. (106)

Rather than taking the reader one step further away from the burning child – Bowie on Lacan on Freud on the father's dream of his dead son – this incisive, imaginative prose cuts through all verbal defences against the dream's pain, and returns the reader to 'the moment of bereavement itself'.

The second kind of writing acknowledges and articulates the impossibility of its own efforts. Discourse of this sort is split between the bold effort to reach beyond itself – to go beyond language in its desire for truth – and the ironic realization of its limited capacity, even in its most prolific moments. Bowie's best example of this overreaching discourse is the Erasmian monologue in Lacan's 'The Freudian Thing':

> ... The Erasmian characteristic that Lacan most admires is *copiousness*, and his manner of truth-telling is often one that seeks to 'say it all' rather than observe literal-mindedly a doctrine claiming that every *all* is a worthless and untrappable prey. Telling the truth, if we pay due attention to the overflowingness of this writing and to its tireless enumerative pulse, is a matter of actualizing the possible forms of the world. An ecstatic sense of plenitude is being sought. Gaps and spaces of all kinds are to be filled. Besides Erasmus, Lacan's kinsmen at these moments are Rabelais, the Apuleius of *The Golden Ass*, and the Joyce of *Finnegans Wake* – those writers who endeavour to capture the transformations of human identity in an endlessly playful and self-transforming literary text, and who propel themselves with abandon towards the supreme moment of abundance that their verbal skill seems to promise. (116–7)

Here Bowie's own writing participates in the plenitude and syntactic propulsion it describes. When criticism and theory are imaginatively energized in this way, they are able to move with the restless dynamics of desire, which is the only way desire as it manifests itself in language submits to being known and registered.

Although Freud appears briefly in the books on Michaux and Mallarmé, Lacan does not figure significantly in Bowie's writing before 1979. At first Lacan is admitted with caution, being given third place after Freud and Proust as a creator of theoretical fictions – for reasons of critical judgement as well as chronology. The myth of Actaeon, brilliantly woven into the argument of *Freud, Proust, and Lacan: Theory as Fiction*, champions Proust's rather than Lacan's version (178). In his Modern Masters volume, Bowie continues to write about Lacan with a determined ironic detachment; but here his refusal to add to the babble of Lacan's 'unconditional admirers' (203) is a respectful recognition of Lacan's own contempt for 'docile mimics' (151). In the version of the Actaeon myth in *The Four Fundamental Concepts of Psychoanalysis*, Lacan allegorizes the myth by identifying himself as Actaeon and the attacking hounds as his sometime followers (188). Bowie, however, neither runs with the pack nor attacks the hunter. Although he celebrates Lacan as 'the only psychoanalyst of the twentieth century whose intellectual achievement is in any way comparable to Freud's', he sees Lacan's 'demythologizing intelligence' as his 'most remarkable legacy' (203).

In *Lacan*, Bowie traces five phases in Lacan's development. From 1936 to 1949 Lacan developed a comprehensive metaphysics, which he later modified or discarded. From 1953 to 1957 – especially in 'The Agency of the Letter in the Unconscious or Reason since Freud' and 'The Function and Field of Speech and Language in Psychoanalysis' (the celebrated 'Rome Discourse') – he turned to the immense task of recreating psychoanalysis by way of a creative and critical reading of Freud. From 1955 to 1964 he developed his triadic model of the symbolic, imaginary, and real orders. In 1958, in 'The Meaning of the Phallus', he assigns the phallus a privileged position in the symbolic order. From 1960 to 1975, despite the completeness of his theory – or because of it – Lacan stresses the dynamic advantages of speech over the language of theory, and works to maintain the vitality of psychoanalytic thought in the face of its institutional and theoretical success, which threaten to make it predictable and routine. Bowie's five phases keep his commentary on the move while at the same time serving to chronicle the development of Lacan's thought. Interwoven with this history, however, Bowie offers his own multi-faceted theory of Lacan's writing and thought.

Lacan is hostile to the language of theory principally because any attempt by psychoanalytic theory to capture desire always leaves something out. Like Freud, however, Lacan is alternately – or simultaneously – anti-theoretical and philo-theoretical. His writing, which refuses to be silent on what eludes it, is militantly difficult, even though it is punctuated by aphorisms that would seem to offer a glimpse of what a full and intelligible psychoanalytic theory might be like. As Bowie puts it, 'Lacan dreams, on the one hand, of merely possible psychologies in a language of overflowing semantic multiplicity and, on the other, of *one* psychology, the only one that would be right, in a language that aspires to simplicity and self-evidence' (4). Bowie points out that Lacan's 'loyalty to Freud is intense, and the originality he seeks is that of an inspired and devoted reader, one who can think fruitfully only from inside someone else's text' (7). Although Freud acknowledged the transience of theory, he celebrated the moments in which theories held together and worked. For Lacan, however, stability and wholeness are illusions. He sees transience everywhere, and insists that 'the disastrous separation of desire from its objects has already occurred' (10). Language, in its incessantly frustrated longing to say what it means, is more than a metaphor for desire. 'For Lacan, psychoanalysis concerns itself above all else with the understanding of human speech, and linguistics, rhetoric and poetics are its indispensable allies' (11). Indeed, Lacan endeavoured to make his theoretical language sound like the unconscious that it sought to describe. Unlike Freud's writing, however, Lacan's is hyperbolic in mode, especially in what often amounts to his overreaching search 'for the extreme form of his own ideas' (13).

Lacan calls upon imagery to do much of the work of argumentation, and in so doing, he creates a text that reactivates in his reader the unconscious processes he is out to recount. In creating his participatory texts, Lacan amplifies theories 'to the point where they become deranged, to supercharge them with meaning in such a way that they no longer have uses or applications' (35). In an explicit echo of Dalí, Lacan sees knowledge as a manifestation of paranoia. Knowledge begins in illusion and misapprehension, 'and constructs an inescapable autonomous system in its wake' (40). In a radical rereading or swerve away from Freud, Lacan argues that the unconscious is available to the psychoanalytic practitioner only in the form of language. Bowie, accordingly, emphasizes the importance of Lacan's 'Rome Discourse' and 'The Agency of the Letter' as key texts in Lacan's thinking about language and the unconscious. The 'Rome Discourse' resorts 'to a style of semi-theoretical incantation in which differences of logical kind are simply talked away' (60), while 'The Agency of the Letter' provides a powerful Saussurean foundation for Lacan's investigation of language and the unconscious. Bowie points out, however, that Lacan's reading of Saussure is no less selective and revisionary than his reading of Freud. Poetry, like polyphony, serves Lacan as a metaphor for the signifying chain, just as his view of literature manifests a controlled ambiguity. On the one hand, poets and critics already know the ways of the unconscious and its language; on the other, they have no privileged hold on language. Lacan's ' "law of the signifier" . . . both binds and liberates; it both cramps desire and sends it on an endless journey' (79).

Since desire, for Lacan, is what 'propels all acts of speech' (122), his discussion of the meaning of the phallus has as its goal an accounting for the intersection of desire and language. The phallus as a privileged component of the symbolic order is gender-neutral, and is based on the embryological conceit of its reference to the primitive structure of tissue that will become either penis or clitoris. Its being under threat is the phallus's most important theoretical quality. In his account of desire and language, Lacan refuses to reduce desire to need. The divided, desiring subject demands unconditional love and affirmation from an other who is none the less divided and can only offer the conditional while also demanding the undivided and unconditional. Despite the technical conceit at its root, the phallus is caught, Bowie observes, in a 'masculinist discourse' that is at odds with Lacan's account of the subject and desire. Lacan's papers on feminine sexuality, which have been translated by Juliet Mitchell and Jacqueline Rose, work to compensate for his apparent refusal to grant signifying power to the female body. 'Where men are energized by the threat of castration and know only the phallic route towards sexual pleasure, women, when they experience pleasure, are empowered from within, "contiguously to themselves" ' (149). Woman is not a universally essential 'all', Lacan insists, because 'for women and for men, "woman" is an endless sequence of projections and fabrications' (151). Nevertheless, Bowie argues, the women who appear in Lacan's writing – from 'Aimée', the patient who figures in his doctoral dissertation, to the Queen in Poe's 'The Purloined Letter' and Bernini's Saint Teresa – are 'patron saints of extremity and indecipherability' (153) with whom Lacan identifies. Women in their *jouissance* guide Lacan back to literature and to the pleasures of the text. Nevertheless, his theories of the splitting of the subject and of language are presented in images that are either without gender or male. From this

Bowie concludes that Lacan offers a prolegomenon to later feminist theory, rather than being a feminist himself.

Despite the completeness of his theory by the early 1960s, Lacan is suspicious of it, insisting that theory does not make anything happen and that the more complete it is, the more powerless. Above all, he works to keep the Other other and to forge a theory that will admit death into its midst. The language and topology of the late Lacan reflect the subject's debasement in passion, the temporal disruption of desire, and death's presence inside and outside speech. In this final phase of his work, Lacan resorts to the disposable graph: the torus, Moebius strip, and Borromean chain. Here 'theory is brought to the brink of its own impossibility' (196). Lacan's purpose, however, continues to be to 'keep on feeling [the] initial shock' of Freud's theoretical texts (196). In so doing, Lacan succeeds in eroticizing the language of theory and in rethinking the complexities of speech in clinical transference.

In the chapter on 'Lacan and Literature' in *Freud, Proust, and Lacan*, Bowie quotes with approval Morris Croll's description of the baroque style in prose: 'It preferred the forms that express the energy and labor of minds seeking the truth, not without dust and heat, to the forms that express a contented sense of the enjoyment and possession of it'(149). Lacan rarely resorts to what Croll calls the 'curt style' (*stile coupé*) that allows no movement. For him, desire is always in transit, language always reaching beyond itself. It is Malcolm Bowie's considerable achievement not only to have rescued Lacan, the master of stylistic and theoretical surprise, in all his baroque energy, from those who would transform him into an immobile icon, but also to have fashioned a prose of his own that clearly glimpses, but refuses to capture, desire in flight.

1 Psychoanalysis and the Future of Theory

'Zukunft' – ich habe das Wort in den Titel meines Vortrages aufgenommen, einfach, weil der Begriff der Zukunft derjenige ist, den ich am liebsten und unwillkürlichsten mit dem Namen Freuds verbinde.

Thomas Mann, 'Freud und die Zukunft' (1936)

(*'Future' – I have used this word in the title of my address simply because it is this idea, the idea of the future, that I involuntarily like best to connect with the name of Freud.*

'Freud and the Future')

The temporality of the human subject as studied by Freud suffers from an internal disproportion that has often been noted but seldom discussed: whereas he describes past time fondly and in detail, his account of future time is foreshortened and schematic. The present in which the analytic subject speaks is poised uneasily, for Freud, between discontinuous time-worlds. The problem lies not in the fact that past and future are logically asymmetrical, but in the seeming flatness that afflicts one of them: the past has character, but the future has none. Romancing the matter only a little, we could say that for Freud the past is 'a character', while the future is a cipher and something of a bore.

My own discussion of this state of affairs falls into two unequal parts. The first and main task that I have set myself is that of describing 'the future' – the concept rather than the tense – as it has been manipulated by psychoanalysis. Here I shall be paying particular attention to the later writings of Lacan, suggesting some of the ways in which his discussion of temporality completes and complexifies Freud's, and pointing to one or two of the problems that this discussion raises for psychoanalysis as a theoretical discipline. 'What kind of future can psychoanalysis have when it talks about futurity in this fashion?' This is the sort of question that I shall be asking in due course.

The second task is that of drawing more general lessons from what I take to be an exemplary moment of crisis in the history of psychoanalytic thought. In this final part of my account, I shall be asking what benefits scholars of a theoretical disposition can expect to derive from attending closely to the 'new' psychoanalytic account of futurity; what new powers of speculation and surmise they may – possibly – discover in themselves when they begin to bring what is not yet the case, what is merely desired, willed, intended, hoped for, or what is merely a matter of obligation or potentiality, within the purview of theoretical reflection. At the very end, I shall spend a self-indulgent moment or two crystal ball-gazing on behalf of 'theory' in a fashion that the approaching millennium has already made into one of the fads of the nineties.

In a celebrated passage from book XI of the *Confessions* of St Augustine, one modern Western view of time is enunciated with commanding authority:

From what we have said it is abundantly clear that neither the future nor the past exist, and therefore it is not strictly correct to say that there are three times, past, present, and future. It might be correct to say that there are three times, a present of past things, a present of present things, and a present of future things. Some such different times do exist in the mind, but nowhere else that I can see. The present of past things is the memory; the present of present things is direct perception; and the present of future things is expectation.[1]

These three times, which are all varieties of the present – the present of the past, the present of the present, and the present of the future – mark out very broadly the temporality that could be called dynamic, or internal, or experiential, or *temps vécu* or *durée*. Augustine is talking about the time-bound human creature, about its powers of retrospection and prospection, and about the internal world of feeling in which those powers are exercised. Against this it is customary to set either the timelessness of the divinity or the calibrated time of the chronometer. Richard M. Gale in his *The Language of Time* (1968) summarizes a familiar distinction when he speaks of two main ways of characterizing time as being, first, a 'dynamic or tensed way', whereby 'events are represented as being past, present and future, and as continually changing in respect to these tensed determinations', and, secondly, a 'static or tenseless way', according to which 'the very same events which are continually changing in respect to their pastness, presentness or futurity are laid out in a permanent order whose generating relation is that of *earlier than*'.[2] On the one hand, a time inflected and made rhythmic by the human being who inhabits it, and on the other hand, a time that is flat, uniform, a continuous succession of temporal points with measurable distances between them. Modal time on the one hand and chronometrical time on the other.

The most sophisticated, and some would say sophistical, modern elaboration of the first of these times – the Augustinian, experiential, modal one – is of course to be found in Heidegger's *Sein und Zeit* (*Being and Time*)

(1927); and in this work futurity is given quite excep-
tional privileges. Where other philosophers often seem
content to think of past, present, and future (*Zukunft*)
as logically and ontologically commensurable notions,
Heidegger presents that-which-is-to-come – the *Zukunft*, as he says, with a playful hyphen separating prefix
and stem – as the home territory of human existence, of
Dasein. He explains his special usage of the adjective
zukünftig or 'futural' in the following way:

> By the term 'futural', we do not here have in view a
> 'now' which has *not yet* become 'actual' and which some-
> time *will be* for the first time. We have in view the coming
> [Kunft] in which Dasein, in its ownmost potentiality-
> for-Being, comes towards itself. Anticipation makes
> Dasein *authentically* futural, and in such a way that the
> anticipation itself is possible only in so far as Dasein,
> *as being*, is always coming towards itself – that is to say,
> in so far as it is futural in its Being in general.[3]

This is an eloquent repudiation of the chronometer in
favour of a temporality appropriate to the impassioned
human subject and to his 'thrownness [*Geworfenheit*]
into being'. We are not talking, Heidegger says, about
a future that comprises a procession of still to be actualized 'nows', but a future that is already shaping
existence in the here and now – one that draws Being
forward towards its fullest realization. What Heidegger
calls 'anticipatory resoluteness [*Entschlossenheit*]' is
'*Being towards* one's ownmost, distinctive potentiality-
for-Being' (325/372).

Heidegger's shape-making and *Sein*-supporting future
is itself a call to arms for a new pluri-disciplinary scholarship. George Steiner has given us an idea of what 'future
studies' might comprise, in the encyclopaedic dithyramb
on futurity which he unleashes in the third chapter of
After Babel (1975):

The status of the future of the verb is at the core of existence. It shapes the image we carry of the meaning of life, and of our personal place in that meaning. No single individual or even culture can produce a comprehensive statement of the notions of futurity. Each of the relevant branches – an ontology of the future, a metaphysic, a poetic and grammar of future tenses, a rhetoric of political, sociological, utopian futures, a modal logic of future consequence – is a major discipline *per se.*[4]

The pressure of Heideggerian futural vision is palpable in this wonderfully optimistic exercise in curriculum planning. From collaborative thought about the existing meanings of the future, a new future in the present is brought into being in the academy. Scholarly *Dasein*, which has familiarly been buoyed up by studious attention to the past, is now to be achieved as readily in forward-flung speculation. Old-fashioned futurists – economic forecasters and thermonuclear strategists, for example – are to be joined by representatives from a whole range of humanistic disciplines, coming together to build a future from . . . the future.

At first sight, the contribution that psychoanalysis can expect to make to such a programme seems severely limited.[5] Psychoanalysis, both as a theoretical discipline and as a set of therapeutic procedures, seems not just to belong to the retrospective rather than the prospective mode, but to base many of its claims to seriousness as a science upon precisely this choice: if you study memories and their repression and the symptoms they produce when repressed, and the mechanisms whereby repression may be lifted and symptoms alleviated or removed, you are studying a continuous sequence of material causes and effects. Whereas if you study merely expected, anticipated, intended, envisioned, longed for, or aimed at states of mind or material dispositions of the world, you are chasing shadows. Besides, those who resort too willingly to future-talk in their quests for meaning are in danger of being facile and simplistic in the meanings they propose. The religious believer with whom Freud constructs his imaginary dialogue in *The Future of an Illusion* (1927), for example, is taken to task for the promptness with which the rewards of the after-life begin to accrue:

> You would have the state of bliss begin directly after death; you expect the impossible from it and you will not surrender the claims of the individual. Our God, Λόγος, will fulfil whichever of these wishes nature outside us allows, but he will do it very gradually, only in the unforeseeable future, and for a new generation of men. He promises no compensation for us, who suffer grievously from life. (XXI, 54)

Where reason works slowly, and under the guidance of a wary and unillusioned hope, the believer's deity works unconscionably fast. The divinely ordained future in which the believer places his trust offers him not merely a retreat from the necessary slowness of rational enquiry but a blissful exit from all temporal process. And a similar regrettable pattern is to be observed elsewhere among apostles of futurity, Freud claims, and much closer to the home territory of psychoanalytic enquiry.

The ancients, Freud tirelessly repeats throughout his writings on dreams, had a profound intuition in seeing dreams as meaningful constructions, and were thus in important ways more advanced than those among Freud's scientific contemporaries who thought of dreams as so much mental noise or somatic 'twitching' (*An Autobiographical Study* (1925), XX, 43). The problem was that the mode of interpretation favoured in the ancient world was the prophetic one.[6] Dreams were pre-enactments in present time of events in time to come; subject to their being analysed with appropriate skill, they foretold the future. Upholders of this hypothesis had a minimal scientific credibility, in that they tried to find sense in places where others did not bother to look, but their guiding explanatory principle brought them into disreputable company. Fortune-tellers, graphologists, occultists, and telepathists, together with representatives of the 'lower strata' and of superstitious 'popular opinion', all indulged in a similar reduction to futurity, and were similarly simple-minded in their handling of complex mental events; neurotics and psychotics did the same sort of thing when they projected on to the future fears and wishes belonging to the past ('Constructions in Analysis' (1937), XXIII, 268).

As a student of dreams, Freud went to considerable lengths to dissociate himself from futurological explanations of this kind. Indeed, in the closing paragraph of *The Interpretation of Dreams* (1900) this essential work of discrimination and self-definition is still going on:

> And the value of dreams for giving us knowledge of the future? There is of course no question of that. It would be truer to say instead that they give us knowledge of the past. For dreams are derived from the past in every sense. Nevertheless the ancient belief that dreams foretell the future is not wholly devoid of truth. By picturing our wishes as fulfilled, dreams are after all leading us into the future. But this future, which the dreamer pictures as the present, has been moulded by his indestructible wish into a perfect likeness of the past. (V, 621)[7]

And although the popular work on dreams that Freud then went on to write is rather more generous towards an opinion that was still widely held, the general attack on superstition is maintained firmly:

> It is interesting in this connection to observe that the popular belief that dreams always foretell the future is confirmed. Actually the future which the dream shows

us is not the one which *will* occur but the one which we should *like* to occur. The popular mind is behaving here as it usually does: what it wishes, it believes. (*On Dreams*, V, 674)

The triumph of the psychoanalytic approach to dreams is that it has constructed a temporality appropriate to human wishes. Where others – Artemidorus of Daldis, say, or the general public of Freud's own day – fatally confuse the time of their own desire with that of external events, Freud in his new doctrine has provided reliable criteria for separating them. The wishful future in particular has a propensity that should prevent it from being mistaken for a simple extension forwards in time of an existing succession of temporal points: as observed in dreams and phantasies, this future constantly turns back into the here and now. For Freud in *The Interpretation of Dreams* the mechanism is clear, and it can be described grammatically: human beings are devoted to the optative mood. This is the time dimension that all desiring creatures inhabit, and 'if only such and such were the case' is its characteristic syntactic structure. This is futurality speaking in and to and on behalf of every human subject. But when subjects dream or phantasize, the future towards which such pronouncements are directed is suppressed. In the dreamwork 'a thought expressed in the optative has been replaced by a representation in the present tense' (V, 534–5, 647). Dreams cancel the future by seizing its desired contents and offering them up to an all-devouring 'now'. Dreams are guilty of a serious temporal fraud, and prophetic dream-interpreters repeat and aggravate the offence.

There are moments when Freud seems willing to grant the future a certain degree of theoretical and even therapeutic importance. 'Past, present and future are strung together, as it were, on the thread of the wish that runs through them' (IX, 148), he says in his essay on 'Cre-

ative Writers and Day-Dreaming' (1908). And it is exactly this mobile interconnectedness of successive wishful
states that brings the patient's future into the consulting
room, and allows discussion even of the remote personal
past to be conducted in an optative frame of mind.
Expectation involves 'a real mobilization of cathectic
energy' (VIII, 197), and to that extent resembles the acts
of memory that analytic therapy sought to provoke. In
addition, Freud discussed at some length, but with little
enthusiasm, the possibility that therapy might have
straightforward prophylactic uses: could future conflicts
be pre-enacted in the consulting room and the overall
duration of treatment thereby be reduced? ('Analysis
Terminable and Interminable' (1937), XXIII, 230–4).
Yet, whatever concessions Freud made to anticipation,
prophecy, and prophylaxis, his temporal balance sheet
was never to become tidy. The past always had a logical
as well as a chronological priority over the present and
the future; and it always had more explanatory force.
The closing gesture of *The Interpretation of Dreams*, by
which, as we have seen, the priority of the past is re-
soundingly asserted, reappears as a motto theme in the
later writings. Even in the essay on day-dreaming, the
three time dimensions are not allowed to hang for long,
in seeming equivalence, on their wishful thread, for
within a few sentences of his fertile metaphor Freud has
added: 'the wish makes use of an occasion in the present
to construct, on the pattern of the past, a picture of the
future [*ein Zukunftsbild*]' (IX, 148).[8] The past supplies
the expectant mind either with the raw material or with
the structural template on the basis of which its futures
are produced; but in either case it acts as an inescapable
destiny. An emphasis of this kind offers not just a slogan
or a watchword for the clinical practitioner: it defines
the entire psychoanalytic approach. In the *New Introduct-
ory Lectures* (1933), Freud reports the opinion of an
'imaginary' analyst that it might be possible to achieve

rapid therapeutic results by consulting only the patient's present motives and expectations for the future. But to work in this way would be to step outside psychoanalysis and begin doing something quite different. 'This may be a school of wisdom,' Freud observes, 'but it is no longer analysis' (XXII, 143).[9]

A number of converging themes in Freud's account of human temporality serve, then, to place the future under suspicion, and to keep it there throughout a long theoretical career. Dreams are not prophecies but wish-fulfilments. They provide not advance glimpses of future time, but hallucinatory annulments of such time. Prophets and fortune-tellers talk about future events in naïvely chronometrical and desire-free terms, and imagine the charm of dreams to lie simply in their allowing us earlier access to a later point in a single untroubled temporal succession. Psychoanalysts, on the other hand, know better than to remove the perturbations of desire from the study of human temporality: while wishfully propelled towards the future, the unconscious nevertheless constantly retrieves that future into the present of its representations. What is more, psychoanalytic explanation proper can never begin ahead of itself, in prospects and potentialities, but only in a materially unalterable past.

We could say, summarizing Freud's views in fewer words than they perhaps deserve, that he consistently diminishes the claims of the future to be of scientific interest, and that he does this in two main ways. First, he postulates an unconscious whose processes know no future time, and have indeed 'no reference to time at all' ('The Unconscious' (1915), XIV, 187). And second, he recommends a method of rational enquiry, available for the study of the human and non-human worlds alike, that grants undisputed causal authority to past events. The unconscious may simply conjure the future out of existence, but the student of the unconscious must obey a stricter code. This obliges him to proceed from earlier material causes to later material effects, to begin his explanatory journey in the past and edge his way forward using archaic events and their residues as his guide. Only then, and only gradually, and only under the shadow of doubt, will a scientifically credible future begin to come into view. It is the analyst's responsibility to study modal time, desirousness, and futurality while keeping his or her own characteristic theoretical procedures quite free of their taint.

One of Lacan's achievements in the post-war period was to build more or less single-handedly a psychoanalytic model of the future. His way of going about this task was in keeping with his general intellectual style, which was boldly acquisitive and assimilative: he reread and supplemented the texts of Freud, fully articulated a past–present–future temporal structure where Freud had provided only a light sketch of one, and drew a number of threads from the Heideggerian account both of time and of discourse into the psychoanalytic domain.[10] The encounter that Lacan arranges between Freud and Heidegger is on the face of it an improbable one. Where the former is devoted to those idiosyncrasies of conduct and speech which, by defining the individuality of individual subjects, act as a bulwark against premature generalization, the latter chooses being-in-the-world, largely considered, as his reconnaissance zone, writes with unappeasable vatic energy, and descends only with extreme reluctance to the anecdotal fabric of daily experience. To be sure, a motor-cycle does appear in *Being and Time* (163/207), but such intrusions are rare. Freud with his 'everyday life' (*Alltagsleben*) and Heidegger with his 'everydayness' (*Alltäglichkeit*) refer us to two quite different conceptions of the mundane world, and seek from that world quite different kinds of anchorage for their arguments. For Freud the 'everyday' is the erotic force

field in which the unconscious makes itself heard; while
for Heidegger it is, at one and the same time, the particular, close-at-hand habitation in which *Dasein* has its
roots and the 'averageness' over and against which *Dasein* achieves its moments of vision.[11]

Yet the encounter between Freud and Heidegger
proves to be very fertile. A preliminary sense of how this
comes about may be had from a joint reading of two
passages that Lacan himself does not align. The first is
a witticism discussed in *Jokes and their Relation to the
Unconscious* (1905). Of a would-be political leader it is
remarked that 'he has a great future behind him' (VIII,
26). There is, Freud suggests, an original plain proposi-
tion in the background here – along the lines of 'the man
has had a great future before him, but he has it no
longer' – and it is by a compression of this earlier form,
supported by a neat prepositional switch, that the shaft
of wit is launched. Here and elsewhere in this book
Freud is of course more concerned with the general
structure of the unconscious as revealed in and by the
play of everyday language than with the analytic encounter itself, in which the playful word is kept within
bounds and subject to contractually enforced supervi-
sion. Yet the joke itself, to which Freud returns later in
the volume (VIII, 214), has the makings of a psychoanalytic precept. For Freud's new science studies not simply
formative and causative events or scenes within the early
life history of the individual, but the futures, themselves
now past, in terms of which such events and scenes were
originally experienced. The history of an impassioned
individual life carries with it, from one watershed moment to the next, a history of the wished-for states by
which that life was propelled. And one obvious lesson to
be drawn from the patient's consulting room narratives
is that the two histories are not parallel but are interlaced
by the language he or she speaks. We need to look
backwards as well as forwards if 'the future' is to be

accorded its full energizing power in the language that therapeutic psychoanalysis employs.

The Heidegger passage that I have in mind sets forth in much greater detail than Freud's explicated joke a comparable pattern of cross-stitching between times and tenses that ordinary usage often seems intent on keeping apart:

> Taking over thrownness [*Die Übernahme der Gewor-fenheit*] . . . is possible only in such a way that the futural Dasein can *be* its ownmost as-it-already-was – that is to say, its 'been' [*sein 'Gewesen'*]. Only in so far as Dasein *is* as an 'I-*am*-as-having-been', can Dasein come towards itself futurally in such a way that it comes *back*. As authentically futural, Dasein *is* authentically as 'having been' [*Eigentlich zukünftig 'ist' das Dasein eigentlich 'gewesen'*]. Anticipation of one's uttermost and ownmost possibility is coming back understandingly to one's ownmost 'been'. Only so far as it is futural can Dasein *be* authentically as having been. The character of 'having been' arises, in a certain way, from the future. (325–6/373)

Heidegger's rhetoric and syntax here are designed to surprise the reader into a new discovery of the elaborate temporal weave that is proper to subjectivity. In the place where you could easily, under the guidance of ordinary propositional language, expect a future that merely lies ahead, just over the horizon of the present, exactly *there* the past, in the form of 'beenhood' (*Gewes-enheit*), lies in wait. Where you could easily, travelling backwards in time, lost in retrospective reverie, expect 'beenhood' and nothing but, there the future has its everyday wonders to perform. 'Die Gewesenheit ent-springt in gewisser Weise der Zukunft': the parting aphorism of Heidegger's paragraph reads almost as a gloss upon the career of Freud's failed public personage, in whose fate we all share. Both writers stand out against

the clock and the calendar, and against those who, un-
duly impressed by these devices, think of desire-time or
Being-time as a simple unidirectional succession.[12]

But Heidegger's segmentation and interlacing of the
temporal continuum goes much further than Freud's.
Past, present, and future in *Being and Time* are the three
Ekstasen of temporality (329/377); each is a 'standing
outside' that is intelligible only in relation to the other
two. To inhabit human time, to be humanly existent, is
to be divided between these outsidenesses, and Heidegger produces much etymologizing word-play between
Ekstase and *Existenz* in support of his claim. But it would
not be right to think of the three ecstatic modes as simply
co-equal and co-operative; for human time has overall
direction, and this the future alone supplies. Being is
borne forwards on a composite tide that pulls it towards
the utmost fullness of being and, concurrently, towards
death, its utmost loss. Time's arrow is aimed unflinch-
ingly at these twin futures, even as the personal past is
revisited and rewoven into the present: 'Self-projection
upon the "for-the-sake-of-oneself" is grounded in the
future and is an essential characteristic of *existentiality.
The primary meaning of existentiality is the future* [*Ihr
primärer Sinn ist die Zukunft*]' (327/375–6). Heidegger's
future in *Being and Time* thus offers a number of separate
inducements to anyone who, writing within the psychoanalytic convention, might wish to revise Freud's own
account of temporality.

From an early stage in Lacan's theoretical career, time
questions play a significant part in his thinking; and even
when his principal interests lie elsewhere – in the causes
of paranoid psychosis, for example, or in the formation
of the ego – the time dimension of subjectivity and
intersubjectivity is often sketched out. In his celebrated
paper on the 'mirror phase' (1949),[13] it soon becomes
plain that, for him, the ego cannot be understood as
gradually emerging through an irreversible process of

precipitation or sedimentation, although memorable images of the nascent ego can certainly be created by using the idiom of natural science. Lacan's account replaces a unilinear time-scale, generated from the relation 'earlier than', by a temporal dialectic, a backwards and forwards scansion. Beware, he is already saying, of any metaphor that promises a steady movement from earlier to later, or from a ghostly premonition of the ego to an entity that is substantial, stable, and self-bounded:

Le *stade du miroir* est un drame dont la poussée interne se précipite de l'insuffisance à l'anticipation – et qui pour le sujet, pris au leurre de l'identification spatiale, machine les fantasmes qui se succèdent d'une image morcelée du corps à une forme que nous appellerons orthopédique de sa totalité, – et à l'armure enfin assumée d'une identité aliénante, qui va marquer de sa structure rigide tout son développement mental.

(The *mirror stage* is a drama whose internal thrust is precipitated from insufficiency to anticipation – and which manufactures for the subject, caught up in the lure of spatial identification, the succession of fantasies that extends from a fragmented body-image to a form of its totality that I shall call orthopaedic – and, lastly, to the assumption of the armour of an alienating identity, which will mark with its rigid structure the subject's entire mental development.) (97/4)

This is the story of an energetic proleptic mechanism that fatally overreaches itself. From within its early 'insufficiency' – its dependence on others and its lack of motor co-ordination – the human infant anticipates the ego that will in due course offer it autonomy and control. But this ego, once in place, proves to be too strong and too thickly armoured for the individual's own good, and threatens to bring a reverse temporal mechanism into play: against the forwards thrust of anticipation a retrospective movement may be established that leads back to the very fragmentation and 'insufficiency' from which the infant had formerly recoiled. Going forward in time to an 'alienating destination' (95/2) brings one to the start of a painful and disintegrative journey back. The rudimentary temporal dialectic mapped out by Lacan in this paper gives us three *Ekstasen* in Heidegger's sense, and at least three ways in which the individual is debarred from any benign sensation of temporal flow: past, present, and future will always stand outside each other, unsettle each other, and refuse to cohere. The future is important to psychoanalysis and its claims must be acknowledged, Lacan is clearly suggesting at this point, but largely because the future, like the past, offers its own distinctive vision of doom.

Lacan's views on temporality begin to extend into the sphere of interpersonal communication in the manifesto 'The Function and Field of Speech and Language in Psychoanalysis' (1953) (237–322/30–113), although much of what he says on the matter at this stage had been anticipated, in a schematic and non-linguistic form, in 'Logical Time' (1945) (197–213). The earlier paper was a detailed re-examination of a logical sophism and, while acting overall as an allegory of the analytic encounter, contained no more than passing allusions to the existing corpus of Freudian theory. 'Logical Time' sought to demonstrate that it was only by introducing the seemingly unmeasurable dimension of anticipation that measurement became possible in the field of human temporality. As recapitulated and extended in 'Function and Field', this puzzling state of affairs begins to yield not simply a way of conceptualizing the intersubjective encounter in its time-boundness, but a way of bringing psychoanalytic practitioners face to face with the temporal paradoxes of their calling.

Lacan works in two distinct registers, which sometimes fuse and sometimes diverge sharply. The first is the 'logicizing' register, epitomized by 'Logical Time' itself:

> l'action humaine, en tant qu'elle s'ordonne à l'action de l'autre, trouve dans la scansion de ses hésitations l'avènement de sa certitude, et dans la décision qui la conclut donne à l'action de l'autre qu'elle inclut désormais, avec sa sanction quant au passé, son sens à venir ... c'est la certitude anticipée par le sujet dans le *temps pour comprendre* qui, par la hâte précipitant le *moment de conclure*, détermine chez l'autre la décision qui fait du propre mouvement du sujet erreur ou vérité.

> (human action, in so far as it orders itself according to the action of the other, finds in the scansion of its hesitations the advent of its certainty; and in the decision that concludes it gives to the action of the other – which it includes from that point on – together with its consequences deriving from the past, its meaning-to-come ... it is the certainty anticipated by the subject in the *time for understanding* which, by the haste which precipitates the *moment of concluding*, determines in the other the decision that makes of the subject's own movement error or truth.) (287/75)

This account of anticipation is based upon the silent comedy of the original sophism, which involves a prison governor and three prisoners. The action takes place between persons, but the mental acts of the characters involved – sifting evidence, reaching conclusions, and preparing for decisive action – are available only by inference from their puppet-like movements. The retrospective dimension that Lacan supplies in 'Function and Field' in order to articulate fully his temporal dialectic is derived from a different – and straightforwardly Freudian – source, but this too is predominantly silent. It is centred on the phenomenon of *Nachträglichkeit* ('deferred action', 'retroaction'), which Freud had discussed in the *Studies on Hysteria* and the posthumously published 'Project for a Scientific Psychology', both dating from 1895, and, more celebratedly, in the Wolf Man case history (*From the History of an Infantile Neurosis* (1918), XVII, 7–122). Freud describes his patient as having received impressions in early infancy that he was able to understand and be moved by only later in his childhood; after a much longer interval, therapy itself caused the now remote personal past to be revived again and further reinterpreted.[14] For Lacan the lesson of these retroactive operations extended far beyond the realm of psychopathology: here was the individual mind restructuring its own past. The Wolf Man had provided Freud with the outline of a process that was constitutive of psychical time, and Freud is congratulated by Lacan on his willingness to articulate that process as a series of transformations undergone by a single implicit structure. 'With an audacity bordering on offhandedness' (256/48),[15] Freud was prepared to remove the event-filled time intervals that occurred between the key moments of the patient's emotional history and to focus his attention instead on an underlying temporal logic. And Lacan logicizes gleefully in Freud's wake. The anticipatory and retrospective axes which extend from every present moment of human awareness are beginning to develop a persuasive-seeming symmetry and interconnection. But something is still amiss if these mute structures are too firmly divorced from the speech-laden practical methods that psychoanalysis employs. The Wolf Man and his therapist *spoke*, after all, and the temporal effects that his case displayed were other than contingently related to the words the two of them used.

Lacan's second register is that of a discourse on discourse. The polemical thrust of 'Function and Field' is clear: if psychoanalysis is a set of clinical practices that have intersubjective speech as their medium, then psychoanalysis should not be allowed to leave that medium untheorized. It is a matter of keeping a major intellectual movement in touch with its founding tenets:

> C'est bien cette assomption par le sujet de son histoire, en tant qu'elle est constituée par la parole adressée à l'autre, qui fait le fond de la nouvelle méthode à quoi Freud donne le nom de psychanalyse ... Ses moyens sont ceux de la parole en tant qu'elle confère aux fonctions de l'individu un sens; son domaine est celui du discours concret en tant que champ de la réalité transindividuelle du sujet; ses opérations sont celles de l'histoire en tant qu'elle constitue l'émergence de la vérité dans le réel.

> (It is certainly this assumption of his history by the subject, in so far as it is constituted by speech addressed to the other, that constitutes the ground of the new method that Freud called psychoanalysis ... Its means are those of speech, in so far as speech confers a meaning on the functions of the individual; its domain is that of concrete discourse, in so far as this is the field of the transindividual reality of the subject; its operations are those of history, in so far as history constitutes the emergence of truth in the real.) (257/48–9)

Moreover, if the encounter between analyst and analysand had a time that was peculiar to it, that time had to be sought and articulated in the medium of speech itself. Speech in the consulting room was future-directed historiography. Seemingly quite suddenly, Lacan departs from his wordless temporal logics: the past and future of the subject can now be appropriately understood only by dismantling the continuous present of his speech and by building the risks and perils of speech into a theory that speaks.

Those who are perplexed by this new emphasis will find an instructive parallel case in *Being and Time*, a work whose phrasing Lacan frequently cites and mimics at this time.[16] After devoting a hundred or more uniquely compacted pages to the question of Being in its broadest and apparent most primordial contours, Heidegger turns for the first time to language. And language, in the form of discourse or 'talking' (*die Rede*), far from being an extension, or a by-product, or an echo, or a far-flung implication, of the matters of Being previously discussed, proves to be essential to their intelligibility. Without language, indeed, those matters would not exist: 'As an existential state in which Dasein is disclosed, discourse is constitutive for Dasein's existence. *Hearing* and *keeping silent* [*Hören* und *Schweigen*] are possibilities belonging to discursive speech. In these phenomena the constitutive function of discourse for the existentiality of existence becomes entirely plain for the first time' (161/204). Hearing and keeping silent belong as much to discourse as do uttering, vocalizing, pronouncing, declaring, and vociferating, and offer an equally precious point of access to the innermost structures of *Dasein*. Moreover, all discourse takes place in the informing presence of others, who may or may not be physically there, may or may not speak, and may or may not permit themselves to hear what is being said: 'Being-with [*Mitsein*] develops in listening to one another, which can be done in several possible ways: following, going along with, and the privative modes of not-hearing, resisting, defying, and turning away' (163/206–7). At moments like these we are preternaturally close to the tone and emphasis that Lacan adopts when addressing his psychoanalytic colleagues on the linguistic burden of their discipline. Language for Lacan is a new 'royal road' to the unconscious, just as it was a royal road to Being for Heidegger. But in psychoanalysis language treads the common path too, and has its full measure of 'everydayness': hearing and keeping silent are basic matters of technique for the practitioner; the 'privative' modes of intersubjective communication need to be examined as a matter of urgency by anyone seeking to understand the structure of the transference; and the failures of analytic therapy, like its successes, are events taking place within discourse.

At present little is known about Lacan's encounters with *Being and Time*, although it seems reasonable to assume that, having read some of it in the original, he received further intimations of its content from Sartre's *L'Etre et le Néant* and from the existential analysts writing under the impact of Heidegger's work.[17] What is known is that Lacan chose to translate Heidegger's lecture 'Logos' (1951) for the inaugural volume of *La Psychanalyse* (1956), and that he there found himself reproducing, almost as an extended epigraph to the new publication, one of Heidegger's most grandiose acts of self-incorporation into the history of Western thought. 'Logos' begins as a commentary on a Heraclitean fragment,[18] but ends as a visionary autobiography. Everything was in place in the pre-Socratic world for the essence of Being to be revealed in the essence of language; yet this did not happen – other than in a tantalizing premonitory flash. Instead, the Greeks launched another view of language – as 'expression' (*Ausdruck*) – upon a centuries-long career that still persists: 'Heraclitus thought the Λόγος as his guiding word, so as to think in this word the Being of beings [*das Sein des Seienden*]. But the lightning abruptly vanished. No one held onto its streak of light and the nearness of what it illuminated.'[19] Just as Heidegger rose to the challenge of thinking the 'Being of beings' in a language that had been devoted to lesser purposes since antiquity, so Lacan presents himself not simply as a linguistically informed contributor to psychoanalysis, but as one who has become the vehicle for a previously unthinkable revelation of *Logos*. The Greek term resounds through his later writings.

The parallel between Lacan and Heidegger is even more striking, however, if we bring the temporality of discourse back into the picture. For Heidegger, discussion of tense and aspect in the linguistic sciences is conventionally phrased in such a way as to suggest that discourse is also, and among other things, about temporal process: temporality is treated as an optional or superadded level of meaning. But this overlooks the fact that 'discourse *in itself* is temporal' and that such temporality belongs to *Dasein* in general (349/400–1). The temporal categories employed by linguists, while remaining useful in other areas of enquiry, simply cannot handle the ontological questions involved. To divide time into three *Ekstasen* is not to conceive of it as a series of discontinuous phases or zones, and not to establish a functional separation between past, present, and future. Whichever would-be phase you seem to inhabit, or whichever tense you seem to have been assigned to by the grammar of your language, you always inhabit all three: '*in every ecstasis, temporality temporalizes itself as a whole.* . . . Temporalizing does not signify that ecstases come in a "succession". The future is *not later* than having been, and having been is *not earlier* than the present. Temporality temporalizes itself as a future which makes present in the process of having been [*als gewesende-gegenwärtigende Zukunft*]' (350/401). What Heidegger is inventing here, in these paradox-laden formulae, is a respiratory system for Being-in-time. The temporality of Being is to be understood as a rhythm that brings together different modes of meaning: as a 'standing outside' that is also an inherence, as a succession that is also an involution, as a continuity that can be grasped only in terms of its disaggregated parts. Lacan is in one sense outstandingly loyal to this way of looking at things, and posits a psychoanalytic subject-in-time who cannot avoid breathing the air of paradox. For this subject, the present is not later than the past and not earlier than the future, because the present is the continual bringing into contact of past meanings that can be restructured but never shed and future meanings that can be restructured but never actualized.

Lacan's central metaphor of the 'signifying chain' readily espouses a general temporal structure of this kind. By way of this metaphor, speech and the silences that punctuate it are pictured as always inescapably inter-meshed with the unconscious and the blanks that it introduces into consciousness: the chain brings together in a single pattern of connections the 'horizontal' axis of speech as it unfolds and the 'vertical' axis comprising the unconscious dependencies by which speech is under-pinned. This desire-driven chain has an unstoppable forward motion, and every present moment of significa-tion, when experimentally isolated from this flow to-wards the future, is found to be a point of intersection between remembrance and expectation. At every such moment 'temporality temporalizes itself as a whole'. But it is exactly here, in his examination of the micro-processes of speech, that Lacan begins to break free from his Heideggerian tutelage. Where Heidegger, in the interests of ontological generality, is concerned not to give too much expressive weight to the time notions enshrined in common speech or in the language of gram-marians, Lacan speaks often, and with apparent grammat-ical nicety, of tenses and of the temporal structures implicit in ordinary predicative utterance. By doing this he maintains contact with the disorderly verbal worlds of the consulting room and the professional society, and takes his distance from the rhetoric of fullness, resolute-ness, and as-a-wholeness with which Heidegger compen-sates for the bafflement and self-division of fallen humankind.

In his 'Remark' on a report by Daniel Lagache (1958), for example, Lacan discusses the power and the sup-posed duplicity of the imperfect tense (678). A sentence such as 'Un instant plus tard, la bombe éclatait' means either 'A moment later the bomb went off' or 'a moment later and the bomb would have gone off'. We cannot know, unless the context is supplied, whether or not an explosion actually occurred. Similarly, Lacan notes, if we say of a mirror image when it has already disappeared 'It was there', we fall victim to the same uncertainty. The imperfect tense provides no existential guarantees; and the verbal gesture that specifies a past presence always specifies a present pastness too.[20] Lacan promotes the future perfect tense in the same way. This tense – by which, say, a desired state may be represented as already having been achieved – brings with it, as an unavoidable penalty, the already-pastness of the very event that has yet to occur:

> Ce qui se réalise dans mon histoire, n'est pas le passé défini de ce qui fut puisqu'il n'est plus, ni même le parfait de ce qui a été dans ce que je suis, mais le futur antérieur de ce que j'aurai été pour ce que je suis en train de devenir.

> (What is realized in my history is not the past definite of what was, since it is no more, or even the present perfect of what has been in what I am, but the future perfect of what I shall have been for what I am in the process of becoming.) (300/86)

The tense structure of the European languages seems to know something important about the fragility of the subject's wishful constructions, and the imperfect and future perfect have a special eloquence on this theme. Indeed, they know more than other tenses about death itself. In his postscript to the 'Seminar on "The Purloined Letter" ' (1966) Lacan introduces a number of schemata attempting to represent the forward thrust of signification in its moment-by-moment progress. But when his playful graphic devices threaten to run out of control, he returns, in order to spell out their deathly purport, to descriptive prose and to tense:

Ceci pourrait figurer un rudiment du parcours subjectif, en montrant qu'il se fonde dans l'actualité qui a dans son présent le futur antérieur. Que dans l'intervalle de ce passé qu'il est déjà à ce qu'il projette, un trou s'ouvre que constitue un certain *caput mortuum* du signifiant . . . voilà qui suffit à le suspendre à de l'absence, à l'obliger à répéter son contour.

(This could represent a rudiment of the subjective trajectory, by showing that it is founded on that form of actuality which contains, inside its present, the future perfect. The fact that, in the gap between the past that it [the subject] already is and that which it projects, a hole opens up comprising a certain *caput mortuum* of the signifier . . . is enough to suspend it upon a portion of absence, and to compel it to redraw the outline of that absence.) (50)

Lacan arranges his tenses in such a way as to produce a death-haunted panoramic view of the signifying process extended in time. At the cross-over point between an untrustworthy past and a promised future that has already begun to decay, a loop, a twist, or a tangle appears within the chain of signifiers. This can scarcely be called 'the present', or 'now', or 'actuality', because at its inception it is already a shrunken and stricken thing, for all the robust play of forces that is to be found inside it. This theme is an ancient one, of course. Marcus Aurelius, echoing numerous Roman and Greek predecessors, characterized just such an insecure and attenuated present: 'One thing hastens into being, another hastens out of it. Even while a thing is in the act of coming into existence, some part of it has already ceased to be.'[21] Lacan's general warning about the sinister intentions that a seemingly beneficent Logos always harbours – 'the signifier as such has introduced the sense of death into the subject'[22] – is ingrained in his detailed account of temporality: time and language acquire their structure from the death's head that inhabits them.

In order to achieve this degree of congruence between the temporality of discourse and the structure of subjectivity, Lacan is obliged to exercise caution in his choice of tenses. The imperfect and the future perfect, which he favours rather as an enraged preacher might favour certain deadly sins over others less potent, produce a much darker model of the intricated present than would the perfect or the past historic on the one hand and the simple future or the 'go-future' on the other.[23] For Lacan there would be little of interest in the tense pattern of such sentences as 'She was happy once, and will be again' or 'He betrayed me, but I shall have vengeance'. In the special conditions of recollection that the analytic dialogue seeks to create, there would be a corresponding lack of theoretical and imaginative bite in such narratives as 'I felt wounded but couldn't work out where the pain was coming from; now I'm beginning to understand and from here on I'll approach things differently'. Lacan does not of course seek to deny that plain future tenses exist and can be efficacious. We make plans and adhere to them, or not; we have obligations and meet them, or not; we sometimes do and sometimes do not pursue the course of action that we have judged morally superior to other courses available to us. And in the build-up to all such acts of commission or omission the various workaday forms of the future tense create an organized temporal context for our choice-making. This tense is vastly unreliable, and may indeed be delusional through and through; yet without it, or another tense standing in for it, we are powerless to choose and to act. Lacan does not deny any of this: he simply removes it all to the margins of the theoretical picture.[24] His selective manipulation of tenses is a promissory, a self-avowedly futural, affair; and the vision it supports is of a future that has already been wrecked. For Lacan all knowledge is founded upon lack, and modes of knowledge that have an intuition at least of this primordial or foundational lack caught up knowingly within themselves are much to be preferred to others. In this general perspective, the temporal conditions of subjecthood can scarcely be other than perilous. If time and language are ever to summon the subject to a sense of fullness – and Lacan does have his own rhetoric of fullness at moments[25] – this summons can be made sense of only by those who are prepared to pass by way of the abyss. All hope is fallacious, and a death's head inhabits our every time-bound word.

I mentioned earlier that Lacan worked in two distinct registers in his attempts to produce a theory of time that was attuned both to the empirical discoveries and to the clinical procedures of psychoanalysis: he was by turns, and sometimes simultaneously, a 'logician' and a student of discourse. The distinction here is between two intellectual styles, rather than between two separate fields of enquiry. On the one hand, he seeks to articulate an underlying temporal architecture for the speech effects that psychoanalysis studies, and, on the other, he re-immerses himself in the hurly-burly of signifying process and in the time effects to which it gives rise. Each of these registers reaches an extreme form in Lacan's final writings and seminars.

One of his major theoretical preoccupations in the last phase of his career was topological modelling of a kind that aimed, by a seeming departure from speech, to reconnect the philosophy of time to the ordinary spoken business of the consulting room.[26] The topological draughtsmanship to which he devoted himself so assiduously towards the end of his life had as one of its principal tasks not the conversion of futurity, or of futurality, into the present tense of 'theory', but the rediscovery of a futurity intrinsic to the structure of the human passions. Topology was for Lacan the consummation of 'logic', but also a way of modelling the characteristic events and temporal rhythms that presented themselves to the clinician.

Everything that I have said so far on Lacan's theory of time might be thought to suggest that he belongs to the Augustinian or 'experiential' party among time theorists. Indeed, we might want to say that all those who concern themselves with the time of desire, or of subjectivity, or of signifying process, cannot be other than experientialists: the interplay of past, present, and future that I have been discussing, and the flexed, syncopated, and paradoxical temporal schemes that I have been sketching, belong nowhere if not to the private-cum-social lives of speaking creatures. Psychoanalysis is a form of speech, and speech the supreme mechanism for organizing human time. I am not sure that this impression of Lacan's views is right, however. For just as Lacan in his theory at large dreams of a perfectly calculable human subject, so in his speculations on time he seems often to want to be a temporal metrician. Chronometers as we currently know them are not appropriate instruments for the science that he envisages. They specialize too narrowly in the simple reading off of successive temporal points or in comparing and cross-checking between separate successions. But he is nevertheless fascinated by the sciences of exact measurement. A Lacanian clock would be one that displayed the unidirectional flow of time while displaying also the spasmodic incursions of past and future into the perpetually forwards-flowing *now* of human passion. Perhaps we are talking about a clock that is also a seismograph – an instrument that numbers the hours and minutes of our life span while recording past shock and future shock too. Lacan's dreams of calculability and measurability in the mental sphere are, among other things, an attempt to create an air of potential or impending certainty comparable to the certainty that Freud had derived from the tracing out of material causes and effects. Where Freud answered those who thought psychoanalysis softly speculative in its procedures by referring to its points of contact with 'hard' natural science, Lacan answered them in an elaborate appeal to symbolic logic and mathematics. Experiential time could be shown to have a firm underlying tense logic, just as subjectivity could be shown to be not at all 'subjective' in the usual popular sense.[27] Troublesome tenses like the imperfect and the future perfect did two things at once: on the one hand, they excited the analytic theorist with their anomalies, and invited him or her to be noisily inventive in his manipulation of time; on the other hand, they revealed the temporal structure of speech as a noiseless bedrock on which speech itself could gain no purchase.

This is one of those points where clinical psychoanalysis and analytic theorizing begin to diverge dramatically. You cannot as a therapist decently confront a suffering patient with a theorem, an equation, an algorithm, or a finely calibrated temporal map of his misery. It is all very well for the theorist to provide himself and his discipline with a mathematicized sense of futurity, but the therapist needs to help his or her patients bring futures to birth in the words they speak. And this means creating and sustaining a spoken language that is diverse, experimental, and prospective. In psychoanalysis, language can never be simply 'futural' in Heidegger's sense – never a simple forward movement of the speaking being towards an anticipated fullness of his or her own speech. The future, as clinical psychoanalysis knows it, is not a matter of free speculative play; it cannot be pursued in a simple utopian or prophetic or apocalyptic mood; it cannot merely erect, in the present, timeless models of what might be or what might cease to be. The future in psychoanalysis is always bound to be approachable only by a retrospective and retroactive route: the only anticipatory gestures worth making are those that the past – rediscovered, recreated, and re-energized in speech – makes possible. The analysand's best and fullest speech is not speech in which the past is simply shrugged off or laid to rest, but one which provides the raw materials and the structural opportunities from which an active, multiform, and abundant sense of futurity can be fabricated.

Those who look into the later works of Lacan for a foretaste of this speech are far more likely to find it in the writing itself, with its astonishing time-teasing syntactic and semantic displays, than in the mathematical and logical schemata that punctuate it. Lacan at his most strenuous and ingeniously playful as a writer uses the technical language of psychoanalysis as a minimal point of anchorage for what are at first sight adventures in polysemy and multilingualism. The following passage, which is drawn from 'Position de l'inconscient' ('Position of the Unconscious') of 1960–4 is characteristic of the rhetorical mode that I have in mind:

> *Separare*, séparer, ici se termine en *se parere*, s'engendrer soi-même. Dispensons-nous des faveurs certaines que nous trouvons dans les étymologistes du latin, à ce glissement du sens d'un verbe à l'autre. Qu'on sache seulement que ce glissement est fondé dans leur commun appariement à la fonction de la *pars*.
>
> La partie n'est pas le tout, comme on dit, mais d'ordinaire inconsidérément. Car il faudrait accentuer qu'elle n'a avec le tout rien à faire. Il faut en prendre son parti, elle joue sa partie toute seule. Ici, c'est de sa partition que le sujet procède à sa parturition. Et ceci n'implique pas la métaphore grotesque qu'il se mette au monde à nouveau. Ce que d'ailleurs le langage serait bien embarrassé d'exprimer d'un terme originel, au moins dans l'aire de l'indo-européen où tous les mots utilisés à cet emploi ont une origine juridique ou sociale. *Parere*, c'est d'abord procurer – (un enfant au mari). C'est pourquoi le sujet peut se procurer ce qui ici le concerne, un état que nous qualifierons de civil. Rien dans la vie d'aucun ne déchaîne plus d'acharnement à y arriver. Pour être *pars*, il sacrifierait bien une grande part de ses intérêts, et ce n'est pas pour s'intégrer à la totalité

qu'au reste ne constituent nullement les intérêts des autres, et encore moins l'intérêt général qui s'en distingue tout autrement.

Separare, se parare: pour se parer du signifiant sous lequel il succombe, le sujet attaque la chaîne, que nous avons réduite au plus juste d'une binarité, en son point d'intervalle. L'intervalle qui se répète, structure la plus radicale de la chaîne signifiante, est le lieu que hante la métonymie, véhicule, du moins l'enseignons-nous, du désir.

C'est en tout cas sous l'incidence où le sujet éprouve dans cet intervalle Autre chose à le motiver que les effets de sens dont le sollicite un discours, qu'il rencontre effectivement le désir de l'Autre, avant même qu'il puisse seulement le nommer désir, encore bien moins imaginer son objet.

Ce qu'il va y placer, c'est son propre manque sous la forme du manque qu'il produirait chez l'Autre de sa propre disparition. Disparition qu'il a, si nous pouvons le dire, sous la main, de la part de lui-même qui lui revient de son aliénation première.

Mais ce qu'il comble ainsi n'est pas la faille qu'il rencontre dans l'Autre, c'est d'abord celle de la perte constituante d'une de ses parts, et de laquelle il se trouve en deux parts constitué. Là gît la torsion par laquelle la séparation représente le retour de l'aliénation. C'est qu'il opère *avec* sa propre perte, qui le ramène à son départ. (843–4)

The passage culminates in a tribute to metonymy, the rhetorical figure that for Lacan is the very emblem of human desire in its insatiable forward motion. The way towards this moment of summation has been prepared by two related puns: on SEPARARE → SE PARARE and, before that, on SEPARARE → SE PARERE. Subjectivity has to do with separation, and also with ornament, dress, decoration, simulation. But the earlier piece of wordplay, on SE PARERE, launches a shimmering parade of witticisms that runs through the entire text: separation is here set against self-appearance, an appearance of the subject for which the subject cannot be held solely accountable, a self-generation that takes place in the eyes of, and at the hands of, the Other and can be conceived only in terms of the otherings, occultations, intervals, and disappearances that it brings with it. These seemingly subordinate verbal echoes and filiations are all motivated by a doctrine of subjectivity as intermittence that is by this period firmly in place in Lacan's teaching: *pars → part → partie* (in its two senses) *→ parti → partition → parturition → appariement → disparition → perte → départ* are a tribute to the intervallic structure of the signifying chain, to the gaps that keep it going. The pun is valued as a sameness that includes difference, as a difference that recapitulates sameness, and as a backwards- and forwards-referring movement in the unarrestable momentum of signifying process.

All the care that Lacan takes to make this specimen section of signifying chain into a visibly and audibly concatenated and self-transforming thing, to make it become what it describes, should not, however, tempt us into understating the firm underlying structure of argument that the passage has. Putting that argument in its simplest polemical terms and remembering the metaphor/metonymy antithesis that Lacan had borrowed from Roman Jakobson, we could say that Lacan is here seeking to promote metonymy at the expense of metaphor: the term *metaphor* occurs only in the highly pejorative phrase 'métaphore grotesque' and the would-be self-replication, the, for Lacan, fatuous cult of self-identity, that this sentence as a whole seeks to indict may be thought of as one of the perils or follies of metaphoricity at large. He or she who merely metaphorizes is trying to create an isolated and timeless island of identity in the time-bound flow of desire. Metonymy, triumphantly displayed at the mid-point of this excerpt, is the desire trope *par excellence*.

A subsidiary argument sets metonymy against synecdoche, with which it is often confused: the conditions of subjectivity rule out any recourse to a *pars pro toto*. The 'parts' which metonymy aligns, and out of which it produces its intervals and its propulsive force, can never be totalized. The *pars* defined in this way has nothing to do with the whole, and all talk of wholes – within the human subject at least – is a ridiculous attempt to refuse what cannot be refused: the scansion, the rhythmicity, the uncompletable, unconsummatable 'processiveness' of desire.

If the quarrel between metaphor and synecdoche on the one hand and an unmasterable metonymy on the other provides the plot for the first half of the passage, the second half is governed by the invisible, sub-textual agent that produced the primary alienation and the endless metonymic displacement of desire in the first place. Lacan names this agent by not naming it, by allowing its or his effects to ripple through the verbal texture. What is the phonemic pattern that belongs in part to these *parts*, *séparations*, *départs*, *pertes*, and *disparitions*, but is not identical with any one of them? It is *père*, of course, but not loudly proclaimed as in the *nom du père* or in the parting gnomic aphorism of Lacan's *Télévision*: 'De ce qui perdure de perte pure à ce qui ne parie que du père au pire.'[28] Lacan's *père* in this passage appears only in the murmuring of the text, dispersed into other words, but encroaching upon all the key terms. He is most explicitly present in the *opère* of the last sentence, and the closeness of this to *ô père* edges us towards the language of liturgical address. Lacan's 'father' is here rather like the dissipated first cause of Valéry's 'Ébauche d'un serpent':

> Il se fit Celui qui dissipe
> En conséquences, son Principe,
> En étoiles, son Unité.[29]

There is a male pregnancy phantasy here somewhere: metonymy is a process of continual parturition for which fathers, not mothers, and fathers to the exclusion of mothers have sole responsibility. Within the phonic substance of this passage, certainly, the divisive legacies of the father – the first destructive *Autre* – are everywhere re-enacted.

But the supremely exciting central thing in this passage is not metonymic displacement itself, or desire, or the scattered traces of the paternal interdict. It is the rhythmic pattern of empty intervals from which the signifying chain, and the human subject, acquire their firm backbone: 'L'intervalle qui se répète, structure la plus radicale de la chaîne signifiante'. We are so accustomed to the stabilizing and mythologizing of individual signifiers, Lacan claims, that we forget the necessary articulating spaces that come between them. Yet those spaces, in their emptiness and in the scansion they afford, are central to our humanity: speech creatures are creatures of the gap, the divide, the lacuna; and if desire has a structure, a principle in terms of which it can be grasped and theorized, that structure resides in an organized procession of vacuities. Desire is not for Lacan an insistent animal appetite, as it often was for Freud: it is what keeps the signifying chain going and what gets you across its gaps.

The decisive interventions of 'late Lacan' in psychoanalytic theory offer at least three lessons to literary studies in general and to the practice of criticism in particular. Each lesson has its own way of making Lacan's account of the future relevant to the desiring transactions that take place between the critic and his or her text. The first would be to follow the injunctions of Lacan at his least textual and at his least accommodating towards the literary practitioner: mathematicize, logicize, schematize, rigorize. The second would be to remain loyal to Lacanian diction – to the characteristic tropes, the tone of

voice, the syntactic upheavals, the conceits and pleasant-
ries – and to stay within the conceptual territory marked
out by Lacan's slogans, key terms, and favourite styles
of argument. The continual danger of this approach is
that of sounding like Lacan's parrot; but the continual
consolation which it offers is that of having the answers,
being in the know, having a system inside which to do
business and battle. The third option – and, as the reader
will have guessed, the one I find most appealing – is that
of learning to unlearn the Lacanian idiom in the way that
Lacan unlearns the Freudian idiom in the passage I have
just been discussing. One of the peculiar virtues of the
Lacanian approach to theorizing is that it does not require adherence to a stabilized and jealously safeguarded
lexicon or conceptual arsenal. Lacan invites theorists of
whatever persuasion to rediscover the pleasures, the mad
exhilarations, of the future tense. In particular he invites
his fellow analysts to come to terms with the prospective,
projective, and proleptic components of their own discipline. He does not, however, use the concept of 'futurality' as an excuse for bland, eclectic rhapsodizing, but
sees it as a call to heterogeneity and boundary crossing
in theoretical discourse. 'The future' as Lacan describes
it is a summons not to 'free' speculative play, but to
inventiveness within an inextirpable framework of constraints, just as the ripple and shimmer of his word-play
in the passage I have discussed is propelled by a sense
of paternal interdiction.

Lacan's lesson to psychoanalysis at large, when he
imbricates the past, present, and future tenses in his
topologies and in his writings, is that it cannot survive
as a theoretical discipline unless it has fecundating contact with discourses other than the one that Freud so
successfully created and codified in the early years of this
century. If it is to shake off the stultifying reductionism
with which it is often charged, it must look to its own
language as spoken in its treatises and in its consulting

room dialogues, and, by way of that language, look to other futures for itself, its practitioners, and its clients.

Learning this lesson is not a straightforward matter, however. We may readily grant that psychoanalysis needs a new and more exacting way of looking at those varieties of future time that its own practices bring into view, yet still not be prepared to think of superior time theorists as *ipso facto* the possessors of superior clinical skill. Discourse may offer us our best hope of understanding the temporality of the analytic encounter, yet still not deserve to be placed at the apogee of clinical experience or of theoretical reflection upon it. Indeed, the temporal effects that analysis seeks to produce and exploit may begin to emerge only when time questions have drifted into the farthest background of the dialogue, or when the language spoken by analyst and analysand has been reduced to a murmur, or to silence. If language is the first and best means of construing time that human beings have available to them, then perhaps the best hope for the psychoanalyst lies not in 'theory' at all, but in the old-fashioned arts of speaking opportunely and knowing when to stop.

How much does the analyst need to know about the paradoxes of the future tense in order to create a forward-flowing as well as a backward-flowing temporal medium for his or her patients to inhabit? Not very much, I venture to suggest, provided always that he or she can remain in touch with the underlying sprung rhythms of analytic speech. For psychoanalysis, while dealing with 'open', or 'contingent', or 'potential' futures of the kind that Aristotle describes in *De Interpretatione* (19a–b), also needs to take a hard-headed view of the historical factors which limit the range of such futures that are available at any one time to any one person. There are practical ways of looking at this combination of opportunity and restriction which, while not claiming to constitute a fully-fledged philosophical or psychoanalytic theory of time, nevertheless make full use of a temporal dialectic of the kind we have been examining. D. W. Winnicott, for example, not only sets forth a general view of play, both inside and outside the consulting room, as occupying a space of potentiality and future-directed experiment,[30] but also provides such 'play' with an appropriately flexed temporality:

The patient must go on looking for the past detail which is *not yet experienced*. This search takes the form of a looking for this detail in the future . . . The purpose of this paper is to draw attention to the possibility that the breakdown has already happened, near the beginning of the individual's life. The patient needs to 'remember' this but it is not possible to remember something that has not yet happened . . .[31]

More recently, Christopher Bollas has written persuasively about the futures that are implicit in analytic speech and about the ways in which the analyst may help the patient to transform a past-driven vision of the future ('fatedness') into a more open and potentiating one ('destiny').[32]

The corresponding lesson that psychoanalysis thus revivified might have for literary studies is that their future needs to be reviewed from the vantage-point of the futurality that each of their procedures implies. Literary theory can prosper, I would suggest, only by attending to the active sense of futurity that is internal to literary language and to the as yet unrealized zones of meaning that inhabit works of literary art. One can think of exemplary works in this vein that happily already exist: Heidegger on Trakl, Blanchot on Kafka, Starobinski on Rousseau, Jean-Pierre Richard on Mallarmé, Freud on Michelangelo, Derrida on Plato, and Lacan on Poe. All these are flexed, tensed, desirous, and prospective critical performances, and all are restlessly inventive in their diction. For such writers about literature the possession of a cogent theoretical viewpoint tends to emancipate rather than confine the language of criticism; all these critical writings inhabit the modal time of the critic's desire, and writing itself is charged with creating and maintaining an urgent sense of interconnection between past, present, and future.

The problem with the 'theory' towards which so many literary critics have gravitated in recent years is that it has seemed to offer them an easy escape from the perplexing time-boundness of the critical act. In certain cases, their commodified 'theory' has been attractive simply because it could still the rage of a literary text, or reduce to diagrammatic form a mobile and overdetermined cultural field. Theory, in this incarnation, is a system of brakes, chocks, and mooring ropes applied to a semantic mechanism that might otherwise – oh calamity! – run wild or fly free; such writing remains safe and normative even as it pays tribute to difficulty, excess, transgression, and catastrophe.[33] Much of the critical language that theory inspires has gone stale, and the time that it occupies is as flat, characterless, and future-bereft as that of a Rotary Club luncheon.

Having reached this point of exasperation with one current state of affairs, I shall now end. I shall do so upon the prophecy that I promised at the beginning. In my crystal ball I see something that positively demands expression in the future perfect tense: by the year 2000 'theory' will have rediscovered art and the threatened but glorious futures that art contains. And art will have been brought back, after a lengthy absence, into theory's own elaboration.

NOTES

1   Augustine, *Confessions*, book XI, trans. R. S. Pine-Coffin (Harmondsworth: Penguin, 1961), 269. On the singu-

larity of Augustine's psychological analysis of time and on the 'inspired crystallisation of his predecessors' ideas' that is visible elsewhere in Augustine's writings on time-related subjects, see Richard Sorabji's *Time, Creation and the Continuum. Theories in Antiquity and the Early Middle Ages* (London: Duckworth, 1983), 29–32, 263–5, etc.

2 Richard M. Gale, *The Language of Time* (London: Routledge and Kegan Paul, 1968), 7. Gale's *The Philosophy of Time* (London: Macmillan, 1968), an anthology of essays (from Aristotle to Dummett), contains a useful section on 'The Open Future' (169–291). For an excellent modern overview of 'The Philosophy of the Future', see David Wood, *The Deconstruction of Time* (Atlantic Highlands, N.J.: Humanities Press International, 1989), 361–83.

3 Martin Heidegger, *Being and Time*, trans. John Macquarrie and Edward Robinson (Oxford: Blackwell, 1962), 373. This passage is to be found on p. 325 of the standard German edition (Tübingen: Max Niemeyer, 1953). *Sein und Zeit* appears as Volume 2 of the Heidegger *Gesamtausgabe* (Frankfurt am Main: Vittorio Klostermann, 1977). (The Blackwell and Klostermann editions both indicate in their margins the Niemeyer pagination.) All subsequent references to *Being and Time* will be given, in my main text or notes, in the form 325/373 (Niemeyer followed by Blackwell translation).

4 George Steiner, *After Babel. Aspects of Language and Translation* (Oxford: Oxford University Press, 1975), 138–9. Newcomers to Heidegger will find a spirited and searchingly interrogative introduction to his work in Steiner's Modern Master volume *Heidegger* (London: Fontana, 1978).

5 Freud, however, had his own futuristic vision of an interdisciplinary teaching and research institution, centred on psychoanalysis (see *The Question of Lay Analysis* (1926), in *Standard Edition*, XX, 246). My quotations from Freud are taken from *The Standard Edition of the Complete Psychological Works*, translated from the German under the general editorship of James Strachey, 24 vols (London: Hogarth Press and Institute of Psycho-Analysis,

1953–74). References to volume number and page are given in the text.

6 What Freud does not fully acknowledge is that 'the ancients' themselves were capable of hesitation as well as superstitious certainty on this theme. Aristotle's *De Divinatione per somnum* begins by raising the very question about the evidential value of dreams that Freud himself was to return to repeatedly: 'As to the divination which takes place in sleep, and is said to be based on dreams, we cannot lightly either dismiss it with contempt or give it implicit confidence' (462b, trans. J. I. Beare, in *Basic Works of Aristotle*, ed. Richard McKeon (New York: Random House, 1941). Although Freud mentions Aristotle's treatise on a number of occasions in *The Interpretation of Dreams* (e.g. IV, 2–3, 33, 97 n. 2, 320n.; V, 550), he is understandably reluctant to see in it any serious anticipation of his own discussion.

7 The last five words of Strachey's translation of Freud's book provide John Forrester with the title for his trenchant short account of Freud's (over-)concern with the possible premonitory dimension of dreams ('a perfect likeness of the past'), in *The Seductions of Psychoanalysis. Freud, Lacan and Derrida* (Cambridge: Cambridge University Press, 1990), 90–6. Forrester points to the kinship between the procedures of the fortune-teller and those of psychoanalysis: for Freud 'the fortune-teller is acting as a wild analyst while remaining completely unconscious of so doing' (94).

8 Even when Freud describes in some detail the mechanism whereby visions of the future are elaborated and sustained, he places his account under the sign of certain or probable failure: 'There are also all the unfulfilled but possible futures to which we still like to cling in phantasy, all the strivings of the ego which adverse external circumstances have crushed, and all our suppressed acts of volition which nourish in us the illusion of Free Will' ('The Uncanny' (1919), XVII, 236).

9 In his footnote to this passage, James Strachey detects an allusion to the teachings of Jung.

10 For a brilliant overview of Lacan's contribution to the

psychoanalytic discussion of time, see John Forrester's 'Dead on Time: Lacan's Theory of Temporality', in *Seductions of Psychoanalysis*, 168–218.

11 For Heidegger's definitions of *Alltäglichkeit* see *Being and Time*, 16/38, 43–4/69 and 370–3/421–3.

12 Heidegger's 'futurality' was already present, in an advanced draft form, in the lecture on *The Concept of Time*, delivered in 1924: 'Dasein is authentically alongside itself, it is truly existent, whenever it maintains itself in this running ahead. *This running ahead is* nothing other than *the authentic and singular future of one's own Dasein*. In running ahead Dasein *is* its future, in such a way that in this being futural it comes back to its past and present' (trans. William McNeill (Oxford: Blackwell, 1992), 13).

13 Lacan, *Écrits* (Paris: Seuil, 1966), 93–100. Page numbers after quotations from Lacan refer to this edition. Where two page numbers are given, the first refers to the French edition and the second to Alan Sheridan's translation *Écrits. A Selection* (London and New York: Tavistock Publications/Norton, 1977). In cases where a single page number appears, the paper is not included in Sheridan's volume and the translation is my own.

14 The bulk of Freud's discussion is to be found in a long footnote (XVII, 45).

15 'Avec une hardiesse qui touche à la désinvolture'.

16 The pattern of Lacan's debt to Heidegger and the interaction of Heideggerian and Saussurean elements in his account of language have been traced, with textual examples, by David Macey in his indispensable *Lacan in Contexts* (London and New York: Verso, 1988), 104ff. Lacan paid a formal, but guarded and tortuous, tribute to Heidegger in his introduction to the German edition of *Écrits* (reprinted in *Scilicet*, no. 5 (1975), 11–17).

17 Our present knowledge of Lacan's acquaintance with the writings and person of Heidegger is summarized by Elisabeth Roudinesco in her *La Bataille de cent ans: histoire de la psychanalyse en France*, 2 vols (Paris: Ramsay (vol. 1), 1982; Seuil (vol. 2), 1986), and by David Macey in his *Lacan in Contexts*. For Sartre's account of temporality, which recapitulates and reworks Heidegger's account in

Being and Time, see *L'Etre et le Néant* (Paris: Gallimard, 1943), 150–218. On Ludwig Binswanger's Heidegger-influenced reformulation of psychoanalysis, see Gerald N. Izenberg, *The Existentialist Critique of Freud* (Princeton, N.J.: Princeton University Press, 1976).

18 B50 in Diels's *Die Fragmente der Vorsokratiker*. This fragment is translated by Kirk and Raven as: 'Listening not to me but to the Logos it is wise to agree that all things are one' (G. S. Kirk and J. E. Raven, *The Presocratic Philosophers* (Cambridge: Cambridge University Press, 1957), 188).

19 Martin Heidegger, *Early Greek Thinking*, trans. David Farrell Krell and Frank A. Capuzzi (New York: Harper and Row, 1975), 78. The German text of Heidegger's lecture is to be found in *Vorträge und Aufsätze* (Pfullingen: Neske, 1954); see p. 229.

20 The two examples are in fact quite dissimilar, and it is alarming to find that context can be usefully enlisted in interpreting one of these twinned propositions but not the other. Even though Lacan's bomb is of dubious grammatical relevance to his case, it has of course an impressive role in his wider campaign to explode the myth of the ego.

21 Marcus Aurelius, *Meditations*, book VI, 15, trans. Maxwell Staniforth (Harmondsworth: Penguin, 1964), 93.

22 'le signifiant comme tel, a, en barrant le sujet par première intention, fait entrer en lui le sens de la mort' (848).

23 The mystery and glamour of the future perfect are emphasized by George Steiner in the chapter of *After Babel* to which I have already referred. Speaking of his own youth, he remarks: 'I found it difficult to believe that the *code civil* put no restriction whatever on uses of the future, that such occult agencies as the *futur actif*, the *futur composé*, the *futur antérieur* should be in indiscriminate employ' (139).

24 In doing so, and in promoting the future perfect in the way I have described, Lacan underestimates by far the modal or 'false tense' uses of simple future forms. Suzanne Fleischman in her seminal *The Future in Thought and Language. Diachronic Evidence from Romance* (Cam-

bridge: Cambridge University Press, 1982) summarizes these uses as follows: 'future-tense forms (in languages that mark future explicitly) are rarely, if ever, employed exclusively for making subjectively neutral (factive) statements, or for posing objective questions about the future. Futures appear commonly in a range of *nonfactive* utterances involving likelihood, supposition or inference, lack of knowledge, wishes and desires, intention and volition, obligation and command' (129).

25 The first numbered section of 'Function and Field' is devoted to the notions of 'empty speech' (*parole vide*) and 'full speech' (*parole pleine*) in psychoanalysis (247–65/40–56). David Macey is surely right in seeing the imprint, in Lacan's usage, of Heidegger's distinction between *Gerede* ('idle talk') and *Rede* ('discourse', 'talking') (*Lacan in Contexts*, 146–8).

26 For a brief account of the topological dimension of Lacan's later work, see my *Lacan* (London: Fontana, and Cambridge, Mass.: Harvard University Press, 1991), 186–96. Fuller details are to be found in Jeanne Granon-Lafont's *La Topologie ordinaire de Jacques Lacan* (Paris: Point Hors Ligne, 1985). The penultimate year of Lacan's seminar (1978–9) was devoted to *La Topologie et le temps*; this forms Volume 26 (as yet unpublished) of his *Séminaire* (Paris: Seuil, 1973–).

27 For a fully articulated tense logic and a review of the literature see A. N. Prior's *Time and Modality* (Oxford: Clarendon Press, 1957) and *Past, Present and Future* (Oxford: Clarendon Press, 1967).

28 'From that which endures of pure loss to that which wagers only from the father to the worst.' (Paris: Seuil, 1974, 72).

29 'He became He who disperses / Into consequences his Principle, / Into stars his Unity.'

30 See Winnicott's 'Playing: A Theoretical Statement', in *Playing and Reality* (Harmondsworth: Pelican, 1974), 44–61.

31 Winnicott, 'Fear of Breakdown' (1963?), in *Psycho-Analytic Explorations*, ed. Clare Winnicott, Ray Shepherd, and Madeleine Davis (Cambridge, Mass., and London: Harvard University Press, 1989), 87–95 (pp. 91–2).

32   In the course of a section entitled 'Futures' in his chapter
     'The Destiny Drive', Bollas, taking his cue from *The
     Interpretation of Dreams*, addresses the following call to
     awareness to his fellow practitioners: 'At the very least,
     then, the dream creates futures, visions of the self in
     transformed states that are nonetheless articulations of
     the individual's unique person. It does not simply gener-
     ate futures, it is vital to the subject's formation of the
     future. It is where some futures are hatched. It is the
     origin of vision, the place where the subject plays with
     objects, moving through potential patterns, setting up
     fields of imagined persons, places, selves and events – to
     be there as potential actuals for future use' (*Forces of
     Destiny. Psychoanalysis and Human Idiom* (London: Free
     Association Books, 1991), 47). On psychoanalysis as an
     *un*writing of the 'fated' future, see also Forrester, *Seduc-
     tions of Psychoanalysis*, 95–6. Adam Phillips writes illumin-
     atingly on psychoanalytic futurity in *Raritan*, 13, Summer
     1993.

33   I know of no prouder rebuttal of 'safe' theory than Bakh-
     tin's hymn to the futurality of the human subject in his
     'Author and Hero in Aesthetic Activity' (*c.* 1920–23), in
     Art and Answerability, ed. Michael Holquist and Vadim
     Liapunov (Austin: University of Texas Press, 1990,
     125ff.).

2 Freud and Art, or What will Michelangelo's *Moses* do Next?

This is not the first, or the thousandth, account of the relationship between psychoanalysis and art. Countless books and articles on this theme already exist; the textual terrain within Freud's own work is extremely well mapped; and anyone who has a modicum of theoretical self-awareness can scarcely avoid having views on the standing of psychoanalysis as a guide to artistic experience.

There are reasons, of course, for the astonishing popularity of the theme, and the market forces governing the dizzy overproduction of printed matter devoted to it can be sketched fairly straightforwardly. Against the sometimes overwhelming pessimism of Freud's more general critique of culture, his reflections on art may be thought of as offering a species of consolation. Let Freud cease for a while being the portraitist of an irremediably divided psyche, the anatomist of our illusions and our discontents, the disconsolate observer for whom there will always be conflict between the desiring human individual and the social order that he or she inhabits, and let Freud the admirer of art and of antiquities step forward in his place. This second Freud wrote at the beginning of his essay on 'Dostoevsky and Parricide' (1928): 'Before the problem of the creative artist [*des Dichters*] analysis must, alas, lay down its arms' (XXI, 176).[1] And this sentence, which has become famous, together with his many occasional tributes to the power of genius in the artistic sphere, have allowed an altogether safe and salutary Freudian aesthetic to be assembled. Freud may have handled certain interpretative tasks roughly and been all but silent on certain artistic traditions and genres, but his overall message is surely encouraging: art is an enhancement of our lives, a partial taming of our savagery, and, although artists are. propelled by passions that retain something of their primitive power and disruptiveness, the work they do on behalf of society is of an integrative and reparative kind. Art is an exercise in sublimation, an attempt to transform and pacify otherwise damaging quantities of affect, but it has a much prouder purpose too: it is the attempt made by certain exemplary individuals to channel their lust, their rage, and their violence into socially acceptable – indeed, commendable – forms. It represents a necessary call to civilization. For Freud, art criticism, in its first phase, takes us back, conjecturally, to the primitive libidinal world and the traumatic landscapes of childhood that the great artist has in part transcended. But then, having visited that world and inspected the artist's wounds, the critic is able, in a second phase, to recreate – the more fully to understand and admire – the civilizing genius of Shakespeare or Leonardo or Ibsen or Michelangelo. Freud as critic infantilizes his artists, but only in order to be able to watch them grow again. He takes us back to the underlying structures – those associated with the Oedipus complex, for example – that their works seem to require and in terms of which the emotional organization of those works becomes explicable, but only in order to watch, with a new clarity of vision, such structures as they ramify and become complex again. On this return journey from the infantile scene and the simple structure, the psychoanalytic critic may nowadays, venturing where Freud himself seldom went, describe what happens when the desire of the artist meets the recalcitrant materials upon which his craft is exercised. The opportunities are legion for a psychoanalytically informed criticism to avoid oscillating simplistically between the complete art work on the one hand and the hypothetical early events that 'explain' it on the other, to observe passion at work upon paint, or stone, or language, or musical sound, and to see the drives of the artist shaping and being shaped by the materials to hand. The critic may still adhere to a systematic psychoanalytic view as he watches the artist taming, or being thwarted or deflected by, the brutish stuff on which he works. The writings of critics such as Anton Ehrenzweig and Adrian Stokes offer luminous examples of this.[2]

All this is fine as far as it goes, and it tells us something noteworthy not only about art but about the special status that art had for Freud both as a theorist and as a clinician. Freud was a cultured man, of course, and his reading, his gallery visits, and his archaeological sightseeing trips may serve to characterize him as a perfect representative of the late nineteenth-century central European bourgeoisie. As a connoisseur and consumer of art, he seldom looks beyond the confines of Europe, but the consensual views to which he adheres, and the canonical works which he admires, speak of a European curriculum of extraordinary range and depth: travelling from one end to the other of the continental land mass, and from the pre-Socratics to Nietzsche and his contemporaries, from Praxiteles to Böcklin, Freud's eye moves from landmark to landmark, and his own intellectual ambition finds a gratifying echo in works that are heroic in scale and execution. Plato, Virgil, and Shakespeare are as naturally his travelling companions in the cultural sphere as Alexander, Hannibal, and Napoleon were in his phantasies of professional self-advancement. But something of far greater practical relevance to psychoanalysis is also going on when Freud confronts his great works: for the student of neurotic disorder and mental impairment, they represent the psychical life lived in a triumphant mode; over and against all the abject and defeated desire that his clinical practice obliges him to examine, they represent desire seeking and exultantly finding its goal. In the work of art the mind of the creator, and to a lesser extent the mind of the recipient, rediscovers the range of its powers – its ability to 'make it new', to produce elaborate structures from simple ones, to contrive its own pleasures, to achieve goals of its own devising. The work of art mattered to Freud, we might say, as a model of successful collaboration between the thinker of thoughts and the performer of actions: by way of art the human being could remove himself for a time from his wretchedness. Clinical procedures would be working well indeed if they allowed a glimmer of this power and efficacy to become possible for the suffering individual. Theorists in their turn have a great deal to learn about their own responsibilities by inspecting the combined complexity and coherence, and the rebellious staying within limits, that great works of art have already spectacularly achieved.

All this is fine, but how far does it go? It tells us very little about what Freud himself actually does when he writes about art, and its implications for criticism are prematurely encouraging. What I shall be doing in the remainder of my discussion is examining three examples of Freud at work on art – as combined critic, connoisseur, and theorist – and then asking what lessons we can draw from a set of interpretative performances that are often dangerously laden with paradox. I shall draw my examples from the fields of poetry, painting, and sculpture, and ask why a thinker who has powerful reasons for taking art and artists seriously, and for deferring to them, should so often write about them in an impatient or appropriative vein. I shall also ask why the practical questions that Freud asks about art have so little to do either with craftsmanship or with the socially beneficial functions to which he pays tribute, but are, on the contrary, partial, obsessed with detail, and tangential to the overall imaginative and emotional impact that works of art, working well, in accordance with his own prescriptions, might be expected to have.

We can get an immediate taste of Freud's strangeness in these matters by looking at his handling of Goethe, whom he so greatly admired, and in particular at the use he makes of Mephistopheles' celebrated 'weaver's masterpiece' (*Webermeisterstück*) speech from *Faust* (Part I, Scene 4). In *The Interpretation of Dreams* Freud quotes this speech in order to elucidate the notion of a 'nodal point' at which a number of dream thoughts converge (IV, 283). The verbal wit and dexterity of the passage from *Faust* are extraordinary:

> Our thought-machine, as I assume,
> Is in fact like a master-weaver's loom:
> One thrust of his foot, and a thousand threads
> Invisibly shift, and hither and thither
> The shuttles dart – just once he treads
> And a thousand strands all twine together.
> In comes your philosopher and proves
> It must happen by distinct logical moves:
> The first is this, the second is that,
> And the third and fourth then follow pat;
> If you leave out one or leave out two,
> Then neither three nor four can be true.
> The students applaud, they all say 'just so!' –
> But how to be weavers they still don't know.
> When scholars study a thing, they strive
> To kill it first, if it's alive;
> Then they have the parts and they've lost the whole,
> For the link that's missing was the living soul.[3]

But the quality of Goethe's writing, and indeed the simple fact that *Faust* is a textual construction, are irrelevant to the point that Freud is seeking to make. What Mephistopheles' artful words are called upon to describe is the earlier, finer, and more surprising artistry that the dreamwork itself possesses. Poetry is silenced, at the very moment of its being summoned up, by the ingenious and inexhaustible mental text that is the subject-matter of Freud's book. Freud returned to this passage in the address he gave on being presented with the Goethe prize in 1930. On this later occasion, he acknowledged that the works of an artist – together with his experiences and 'instinctual endowments' (*Triebanlagen*) – belonged to the busy weaving shop of his mental activity; but he was still reluctant to furnish even the most celebrated of those works with additional characteristics (XXI, 212). Art works had no arresting oddities of texture or coloration, and the production processes from which they emerged were not peculiar to them. Indeed, Goethe is praised throughout the address for his profound knowledge of the human mind and for the pre-psychoanalytic prescience of that knowledge, rather than for his achievements as a writer.

The thinning out of the category 'literature' in *The Interpretation of Dreams* is particularly strange, because the text of that book is saturated with literary references, and because interpretation of a gleeful and insistent kind is brought to bear upon everything else in sight. Novels, poems, and plays are extensively quoted and alluded to: they supply fodder for the dreams of literate persons; they provide bridges, switches, nodal points, punctuation marks, philosophical observation platforms, and numerous other aids to the act of dream interpretation; and they map out the encompassing cultural space in which these *fin-de-siècle* dreams and their interpretations alike unfold. But, with the exception of an excursus here or there, literary texts are not themselves interpreted. Dreams are authentically beautiful, and literature merely provides that beauty with certain of its adventitious ornaments. None of this is odd if Freud's project in his dream book is returned to its historical moment. If dreams demand interpretation whereas literature does not, this is largely because the intellectual dignity of dreams still has to be fought for by Freud, whereas the credentials of literature are already complete and beyond question.

Freud's skills as an interpreter are nowhere more evident than in the copious discussion of his own dreams that forms the backbone of *The Interpretation of Dreams*. It is here that the student of literature and of the other arts will find psychoanalysis confidently promoted as a general science of interpretation, and here too that its lessons for criticism become especially difficult to construe. These dreams, their associations, and the analyses to which they are submitted comprise a pained and exultant farewell ceremony for Freud's father, who had recently died. As an example of Freud's hermeneutic audacity, I have chosen from among them the dream involving Count Thun, which is also known as the 'Revolutionary Dream' (IV, 208ff., and V, 432ff.).

This dream, triggered in part by the sight of Franz Anton Thun, who had been Austrian prime minister in 1898–9, takes us into an Austro-Hungarian fantasy world reminiscent of Schnitzler, Musil, and Kraus. And if there were not so many other reasons for thinking the dream, its associations, and its interpretation remarkable, one could take detailed note of the astonishing parade of artistic references and allusions that Freud has packed into his account.[4] In the space of a few pages we meet Mozart, Beaumarchais, Tennyson, Italian architecture, Shakespeare's *Henry VI*, Zola's *Germinal* and *La Terre*, Grillparzer, Rabelais, Norse and Greek mythology, Spanish popular song, and much more. These references overspill the text into long footnotes, and accumulate so fast and in such a reckless polyglot fashion – there are quotations in four European languages other than

German – that we seem to be drawing close to the exhaustive intertextual and interlingual dream world of Joyce's H. C. Earwicker in *Finnegans Wake*. Freud's reading of the dream narrative contains numerous other associative flights, at the level both of word-play and of historical and personal reminiscence. But what is more remarkable, it seems to me, than this constant air of semantic overflow and dispersal is Freud's insistence upon parsimony in his interpretative procedures. The dream of Count Thun is given as an example of apparent absurdity in dreams, and Freud is intent upon articulating the underlying logic that such dreams must, according to the argument of his book, possess. The fundamental associative principles involved in the interpretation of dream material are two only, condensation and displacement, and each of these principles operates in a twofold manner: upon words and upon ideas. A similar economy is at work in the organization of the emotional content of the dream: Freud as dreamer is at one moment a reactionary German nationalist (rather like Thun) and at another a rebellious Hispano-Franco-Italian underling like Mozart and Da Ponte's Figaro (in his preamble, he quotes 'Se vuol ballare, signor contino') (IV, 208–11); he is both modest and arrogant, a person of ambition and a person of none; he shows filial respect towards his father, but also filial vengefulness and spite. Here is the individual dreaming mind become the site of a tragic drama interspersed with farcical episodes, and the same mind self-divided into a complete *dramatis personae*. Yet Freud is not celebrating a purely egotistical mystery, or the multiplicity of a mere private self. The social and political tensions and discords that he internalizes in analyses like this one are set out in appropriately discriminating social and political terms: the dream and its analysis are a psychical monodrama that is not just scrupulously connected up to ambient Austro-Hungarian society, but is shown to be, in its circumstantial unfolding, a product of that society.⁵ There is no short cut to the prototypical structures that make even the craziest-seeming dreams intelligible. The route that leads 'back' or 'down' to those structures takes the interpreter through a maze of circumstances, which includes that of having read certain books but not others.

The interpretative procedures to be seen at work in a performance such as this cannot readily be expressed in terms of the familiar circles and spirals of an earlier German hermeneutic tradition. A more useful series of figures for what is going on in Freud's analysis would be those of explosion/implosion, expansion/contraction, or dispersal/concentration. A finite quantity of observational material is being worked upon (a dream narrative), and a more than just finite – a severely and conscientiously restricted – set of analytic principles is being applied to it. But that material becomes unruly as soon as its associations are unleashed: its previously contained semantic energies burst forth in sudden moments of *éclat*. And then, when the scattered self has become a population of selves and the analytic intelligence has reached its point of vertigo, the explosion is contained and reversed by reference to the simple structures and the simple emotional truths held to underlie the activities of the dreamwork: condensation versus displacement, Thun versus Figaro, hostility versus tenderness. The combined permissiveness and self-restriction of Freud's interpretations provide an exhilarating, though not easily reproducible, object-lesson for all those who have truck with literary criticism. He travels long distances upon the signifying ocean, yet remains dogged, trenchant, and precise in his explanations of the world. He is lured towards Finneganism and Earwickerdom, yet continues to heed the imperious call of science.

The *time* of interpretation is at least as complex as the space of its intersecting associative networks. The alternating dispersal and concentration of the interpretative imagination that are to be seen in Freud's discussion of the Thun dream establish a broad temporal rhythm; but inside this, a much more finely calibrated temporality is also to be observed. From the first paragraph of commentary on the dream text, time intervals are spelled out with anxious precision:

> The dream as a whole gives one the impression of being in the nature of a phantasy in which the dreamer was carried back to the Revolutionary year 1848. Memories of that year had been recalled to me by the [Emperor Francis Joseph's] Jubilee in 1898, as well as by a short trip which I had made to *the Wachau*, in the course of which I had visited Emmersdorf, the place of retirement of the student-leader Fischhof, to whom certain elements in the manifest content of the dream may allude. My associations then led me to England and to my brother's house there. He used often to tease his wife with the words 'Fifty Years Ago' (from the title of one of Lord Tennyson's poems), which his children used then to correct to '*fifteen years* ago'. This revolutionary phantasy, however, which was derived from ideas aroused in me by seeing Count Thun, was like the façade of an Italian church in having no organic relation with the structure lying behind it. But it differed from those façades in being disordered and full of gaps, and in the fact that portions of the interior construction had forced their way through into it at many points. (IV, 211)

The associative fabric that Freud offers his reader here is one of alarming historical instability. Any point in past time that is supplied as a member of an emerging time sequence may bring with it its own further increment of pastness, and of past futurity. Freud returns to the eighteenth century in order to find, in Figaro, an emblem of his own inner rebellion against a brutish aristocracy. But he finds a future as well as a past in the lines he has already quoted from Act I of *Le Nozze di Figaro*:

Se vuol ballare, signor contino
Il chitarrino, le suonerò.

Freud and Figaro meet, and together defy their respective counts, in 'the Revolutionary year 1848': the one
travels back in time as the other travels forward. All
temporal simples turn into compounds in this way. The
date 1898 becomes intelligible by reference to 1848, and
the relation between the two dates is rethought in terms
of the contiguity between an earlier and a later architec-
tural style. The 'fifty years ago' mentioned by Freud's
brother (and possibly derived from a misremembering of
Tennyson's 'Locksley Hall Sixty Years After') is reduced
by his brother's children to 'fifteen years ago'. Austrian,
English, and Italian time-scales intersect. The past is
irreducibly composite, freighted with earlier or alternative pasts, and always shot through with future-directed
intention and surmise. Retrospection and anticipation
are latent in every particle of the desiring subject's history. The temporal micro-rhythms that appear in this
preliminary working through of the dream's associations
reappear in the analysis proper, and indeed this analysis
soon develops its own plot and its own power of temporal
self-reference.

Freud was acutely conscious of the need to separate
the sober constructions of the dream-interpreter from
the wishful content of the dream narratives upon which
he exercised his skill. Where desire belonged to the sub-
junctive and optative moods, interpretation was honour
bound to adhere to the indicative. It was upon the patient
sequential tracing out of mental causes and effects that
the scientific claims of psychoanalysis rested, and to this
end the grammar of interpretation had to be purged
of merely wish-bearing constructions. Professional prudence, one might have imagined, would make Freud
particularly careful when it came to the temporal organization of his own text: dreams may cheat with the

centuries, but analysis may not; dreams may have an unstable and involuted time-scale, but analysis, in the name of science, must be made of sterner and straighter stuff. It should not come as a surprise to find that Freud is imprudent and 'unscientific' in the handling of his own dreams, for this material springs from a singular moment of upheaval in his affective life. What is perhaps surprising is that his main accounts of art and artists should also run counter to his notions of intellectual rectitude, and develop their own wayward interpretative pulse.

Freud's essay *Leonardo da Vinci and a Memory of his Childhood* (1910) is organized by the pattern of concentration and dispersal that I described earlier. On the one hand, the work of art is immobilized upon an isolated feature: the smile of the Mona Lisa or the redoubled presence of smiling womanhood in the *Virgin and Child with Saint Anne*, which are to such an extent the primary matters to be explained in their respective paintings that Freud's critical attention begins to lapse as soon as an appropriate key to their mystery has been found in Leonardo's childhood memory. A single feature, thus privileged, keeps all the other meanings of the work in check, if it does not actively exclude them. On the other hand, when Leonardo's career and creative personality come to occupy the foreground of discussion, Freud recreates in the mobile textures of his own writing the varied fortunes of the *Wißtrieb*. Tribute is paid to Leonardo as a heroic embodiment of the 'drive to know' and as one in whom curiosity and experimentation are constantly threatened by brooding and self-doubt. Freud re-stages this dramatic conflict in a prose that seeks to reinhabit the artist's working space and rediscover from different angles the invariant substructure of his thinking. Here, for example, he recapitulates Leonardo's creative life as one grandiose spasm of the feeling intellect:

During this work of investigation love and hate threw off
their positive or negative signs and were both alike
transformed into intellectual interest. In reality Leonardo was not devoid of passion; he did not lack the
divine spark which is directly or indirectly the driving
force – *il primo motore* – behind all human activity. He
had merely converted his passion into a thirst for
knowledge [*Wissendrang*]; he then applied himself to
investigation with the persistence, constancy and
penetration which is derived from passion, and at the
climax of intellectual labour, when knowledge had been
won, he allowed the long restrained affect to break loose
and to flow away freely, as a stream of water drawn from
a river is allowed to flow away when its work is done.
When, at the climax of a discovery, he could survey a
large portion of the whole nexus, he was overcome by
emotion, and in ecstatic language [*in schwärmerischen
Worten*] praised the splendour of the part of creation that
he had studied, or – in religious phraseology – the
greatness of his Creator. (XI, 74–5)

This is a discreet account of the sexual drive as it under-
goes a double transformation: the sexual researches of
the child have become the adult's equally impassioned
epistemic quest, and that quest, at its moment of fulfilment, has issued in a religious sense of rapture and
wonderment. Freud is more than simply patient with
sublimatory movements of this kind, for without them
the monuments of human civilization that he so much
prizes would not exist. He allows a 'divine spark' to set
things going, and re-uses Leonardo's language of awe
and reverence when he describes the blissful outcome of
the desire to know. Understanding the mental mechanism known to psychoanalysis as *sublimation* does not
make the achievements of Leonardo any less sublime.
Those achievements are no less exalted, and no less
driven by an ecstatic futural vision, for having begun life
in the sexual bafflement of a young child. But at the
same time psychoanalysis cannot prosper, or maintain

its individuality as an intellectual method, if it attends simply to a supposed unidirectional flow of time or meaning. It must desublimate the work of culture as well as acquiesce in its progressive self-removal from the infantile scene. It must go back in order to go forward. In this passage the responsibility for introducing into the picture a still active past and a still primordial and un-sublimated sexual energy is given to the central imagery of climactic discharge: here the *Wißtrieb* has been re-turned to its point of origin in the excitable tissues of a pleasure-seeking organism. Artistic and intellectual en-deavour have rejoined the hydrodynamic force field of nature. Sex and knowledge have been reunited in a pri-mal dampness.

What is remarkable in passages like these is the intens-ity with which Freud seeks to relive the entire existential project of his subject. Leonardo's artistic and scientific activities are all envisaged in the medium of time; but this is not because complicated tasks take time to per-form, or even because the path towards a scientific dis-covery or a finished work of art is littered with discarded drafts and sketches. Freud's exemplary creative individ-ual inhabits a time that is always simultaneously past-haunted and future-haunted. He suffers from memories, and from cataclysmic visions of the future. His ecstasy comes not as an escape from this tension, but as a defiant manipulation of it. The past – surveyed, fa-thomed, herded, reined in – is the living precondition for the forward-flung motions of his intelligence. And beneath the inflected surface of any individual creative project the underlying life project remains visible. Freud repeats the story of Leonardo's drive for knowledge; he repeatedly sets the privations of a childhood against the abundant inventiveness of a singular adult mind; he watches culture as it emerges from the interplay of natu-ral energies and as it dissolves back into a nature that it can never fully control. From these constant dialectical shifts and repositionings, a model of time-bound and matter-bound speculative activity is built to which Leonardo and Freud himself can both subscribe.

The rhythm of concentration and dispersal to be found in the Leonardo essay is unusual in one respect: from an extremely parsimonious set of causes springs a glittering array of effects. Few works of art are discussed, and those from the viewpoint of certain details only; few of Leonardo's childhood memories are available for discussion, and of these only one is considered at length. But on the basis of these tiny nuclei of information and hypothesis, an entire vision of intellectual creativity is conjured into being. It is characteristic of psychoanalysis, Freud claims on numerous occasions, that it should see meaning in details that other kinds of thinking systematically ignore. For the psychoanalyst 'nothing is too small to be a manifestation of hidden mental processes' (XI, 119). But the extraction of meaning from detail is fuelled here by much less material than Freud requires in his case histories and dream interpretations. Under the benign influence of a great artist, an explanatory magic is at work.

In the paper on Michelangelo's *Moses* that Freud published, anonymously, four years after his *Leonardo*, this cult of the pregnant detail is pursued even more vigorously.[6] Indeed, in this essay, to which I shall devote the remainder of my discussion, 'despised or unnoticed features, from the rubbish-heap, as it were, of our observations' (XIII, 222) are dwelt upon seemingly at the expense of psychoanalytic explanation as Freud had previously defined it. Such crucial psychoanalytic notions as the unconscious, repression, and drive are present here only as pale shadows, and the *explicanda* that Freud lists in his opening pages have little to do with psychopathology. Freud pays special tribute to the Italian physician, politician, and art critic Giovanni Morelli (1816–91), whose reputation rests upon one outstanding contribution to connoisseurship and the science of attribution.[7] Look at the way a given artist paints such ordinary things as ear lobes or finger-nails, Morelli urged, and you will discover the distinctive imprint of his style. Followers, imitators, and forgers can be caught red-handed by their inability to reproduce such stylistic effects at the threshold of what is visible in a painting. Freud's argument in 'The Moses of Michelangelo' (1914) is concerned precisely with the reinterpretation of certain key details, and is presented as an amateur's minor contribution to art history. Morelli and Freud are allies, looking at art with the same sort of vigilance and suspicion. No new lessons for psychoanalytic theory or practice are to be drawn from Freud's exploration.

Freud had many reasons for taking Michelangelo's statue seriously and for returning to it during his frequent visits to Rome. These reasons have often been rehearsed: the figure of Moses was a reminder in marble of the centrality that patriarchal authority had in Freud's own doctrine; it was a grand Judaic emblem rising up within the iconography of Christian Rome; it allowed Freud to examine in himself those ambivalences towards Judaism and Jewish tradition that were to appear again, and still more dramatically, in *Moses and Monotheism* (1939); and it provided him with a supreme image of the prophetic truth-teller standing out against a decadent and deluded collectivity. But if we set aside for a moment the many ways in which Freud was able to identify with the sculptor and his subject, we are entitled to ask two questions in the suspicious mode that Freud praised in Morelli, and thereby to bring two of the essay's own 'insignificant details' (XIII, 235) into focus. Why was the essay published anonymously? Why did Freud stitch so much of it together from lengthy quotations from earlier writers whose views he did not share? This double self-absenting from the responsibilities of authorship seems especially strange when one remem-

bers the straightforward heroic ambitions that many
commentators on the essay have ascribed to its author.
I shall return to these questions in due course.

Those who still worry about the 'intentional fallacy',
and who are made additionally nervous by the string of
tu quoque charges that Wimsatt and Beardsley's famous
paper[8] has provoked over the decades, are likely to find
a certain antediluvian charm in the general critical atti-
tude that Freud adopts in discussing Michelangelo.[9] For
here is 'intentionalism' pure and unashamed:

> what grips us so powerfully [in great works of art] can
> only be the artist's *intention* [*Absicht*], in so far as he has
> succeeded in expressing it in his work and in getting us
> to understand it. I realize that this cannot be merely a
> matter of *intellectual* comprehension; what he aims at is
> to awaken in us the same emotional attitude, the same
> mental constellation as that which in him produced the
> impetus to create. But why should the artist's intention
> not be capable of being communicated and compre-
> hended in *words*, like any other fact of mental life? (XIII,
> 212)

Freud writes movingly about the labour of interpretation
that is required if an intention that has already had its
emotional effect upon the recipient is to be fully understood. 'My duty was to see more clearly into my delight,'
Proust's narrator says, to explain why a richer verbal
response than 'Zut, zut, zut, zut' was required to an unusual pattern of reflected light.[10] And Freud's recourse to
interpretation is of the same kind. It involves a passage
through writing towards a new and deeper absorption
in the seemingly wordless rapture that artistic experience brings. The intention of the artist, expressed in
the work and then patiently reconstructed by the interpreter, is at once the source of aesthetic pleasure and a
guarantee of the work's intelligibility. It is the place
of origin to which any exegetical procedure – however

elaborate and self-delighting it may become – should finally return us.

Freud's preamble, therefore, is devoted to the mind of Michelangelo, and the intentional structure of that mind provides Freud's later interpretation with a necessary backstop. At this point he could have begun to consider directly the formal properties of the statue, treating them as the best available evidence for the artist's wishes. But Freud chooses not to do this. What he goes on to provide is a further glimpse into a lost mental world and a deeply problematic further variety of intentionalism. He devotes the bulk of his essay to the mind not of Michelangelo, but of Moses himself, and considers only those properties, or 'insignificant details', that appear to reveal it. One question occupies the centre of the stage: what will Moses do next? Previous scholarly debate, as summarized by Freud, is entirely concerned with this vexatious problem, and his own argument is directed, in friendly competition with other commentators, towards a new, improved solution.

First of all, Freud gives the generally accepted view: 'In the next instant Moses will spring to his feet – his left foot is already raised from the ground – dash the Tables to the earth, and let loose his rage upon his faithless people' (XIII, 216). He then lists and quotes those authorities who have espoused this view in one form or another, showing particular warmth towards the writers who have gone furthest in the psychological – and indeed physical – animation of a stationary figure. All the critics cited provide Moses with a future as well as a present and a past, but two of them earn Freud's particular praise. These are Justi, who writes:

> in the next instant he will leap up, his mental energy will be transposed from feeling into action, his right arm will move, the Tables will fall to the ground, and the shameful trespass will be expiated in torrents of blood.

and Knapp, in whose account a lively sound-track connects the three temporal *ecstases*:

> He hears a noise; the noise of singing and dancing wakes him from his dream; he turns his eyes and his head in the direction of the clamour. In one instant fear, rage and unbridled passion traverse his huge frame. The Tables begin to slip down, and will fall to the ground and break when he leaps to his feet and hurls the angry thunder of his words into the midst of his backsliding people. (XIII, 218)

These are wrong answers to the question 'What next?', but the fact that there is something 'extraordinarily attractive about attempts at an interpretation of the kind made by Justi and Knapp' (XIII, 219) suggests that there is perhaps something profoundly right about them too. These critics have looked at the detail, read the signs, and on this basis entered a world of coherently unfolding temporal process. They have discovered something important about the way intentions are organized and about the way in which they organize in their turn the flow of human time. Justi and Knapp, for all their novelettish excesses, have discovered the backwards-and forwards-looping movement of desire-time. From an incursion of pastness into Moses' present – the memory of his own calling and of what the tables ordain – a mighty future deed is gathering force and form. When Freud moves on, after further delays, to his own solution, this involuted temporal structure is preserved intact. More than a mere nicety of critical reading is clearly at stake.

Freud argues that Moses, far from propelling himself into violent action, is embarking upon a future of hard-won self-restraint and philosophic calm. Michelangelo

> has added something new and more than human to the figure of Moses; so that the giant frame with its

tremendous physical power becomes only a concrete
expression of the highest mental achievement that is
possible in a man, that of struggling successfully against
an inward passion for the sake of a cause to which he
has devoted himself. (XIII, 233)

This bold reversal of a commonplace view is arrived at
not by introducing fresh material evidence, but by re-
interpreting two details that had already been exhaustively
discussed in the literature: the position of Moses' right
hand in and against his abundant beard and the position
of the tables beneath his right arm. Where others had
seen indignation and wrath building up in the play of
fingers and beard, Freud sees these same emotions being
calmed: the fingers leave a diminishing wake behind
them, and speak of an impulse to action that is gradually
being abandoned. Where others have found the tables
awkwardly poised and dangerously close to falling,
Freud finds them newly secured and protected. The
proponents of each view are in agreement that these
details together furnish an essential time map within an
otherwise static design: the map is ambiguous, but the
secret of the work's dynamism, and of its temporally
extended moral drama, is to be found somewhere upon it.

Freud reaches in two quite separate ways towards the
ungraspable inner toil of Moses' feelings. First, over
several rapturous pages, he re-manipulates the manipul-
ating hand, and sketches a new science of capillary
motion in his descriptions of the beard:

At the place where the right index finger is pressed in,
a kind of whorl of hairs is formed; strands of hair coming
from the left lie over strands coming from the right, both
caught in by that despotic finger. It is only beyond this
place that the masses of hair, deflected from their
course, flow freely once more, and now they fall vertic-
ally until their ends are gathered up in Moses' left hand
as it lies open on his lap. (XIII, 223)

And there is much more in the same vein. The undulating excess of this writing suggests that Freud has found, in the whorls and vortices of the beard, not simply a clue to artistic meaning, but a key to the structure of the natural world, a wave principle governing everything. In writing like this it is no longer a matter of eliciting 'a clear and connected sequence of events' (XIII, 225) or a single temporality for the Moses story, but of turning time into textually manipulable stuff. The beard, while leading the interpretative imagination outwards to a single grand informing meaning, is also a concentrate of small-scale temporal effects, a hirsute topological space.

But secondly, Freud, in search of Moses' inwardness, went to unusual lengths to narrativize the statue. He commissioned an artist to draw the figure in the hypothetical former states that his new interpretation seemed to imply. He guessed, and someone else drew his guesses. What the two of them produced, however, was a critique of sculpture conducted from the viewpoint of a minimalist cinematography. In three successive frames, the complete history of an event has been told: an intention has been provoked, followed through to the beginnings of action, and then abandoned. But although the event has its own characteristic shape and may be removed from the temporal continuum for experimental purposes, other events may be added to it indefinitely, in either direction. Moses may be pictured receiving the tables in an earlier past than that of figure 1 or wisely counselling his errant people in a later future than that of figure 3. Solid marble has been melted into the airy element in which prophets and interpreters alike do their thinking.

Freud presents us, then, with two temporalizations of Michelangelo's work. The first, derived from Justi and Knapp and only reluctantly discarded, involves a special intrication of past, present, and future time, and brings together in a composite portrait the psychological

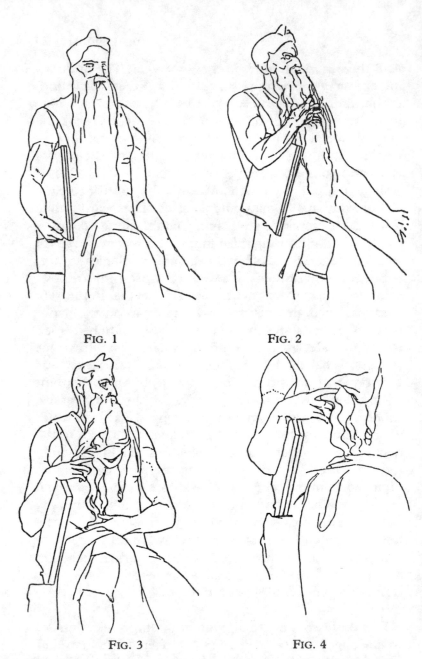

FIG. 1

FIG. 2

FIG. 3

FIG. 4

Figures 1–4. Drawings commissioned by Freud for 'The Moses of Michelangelo' (By courtesy of Hogarth Press and Institute of Psycho-Analysis).

motions of Moses himself, his sculptor, the average vis-
itor to San Pietro in Vincoli, and the critic as exemplary
spectator. The second, argued for with passion, involves
the same involution of time and the same cast of actors.
The difference between them has to do simply with the
locus of future action. In the first case, we move from
the world of·feeling into that of public behaviour: Moses
is moved to violent protest against the worship of idols.
In the second, we remain inside a mind: action is ruled
out as fisticuffs, and continued, sublimely, as thought.
The two interpretations are the same temporal structure
in different psychological clothes. Yet, although the two
readings are irreconcilable and presented as such, their
tendency is of course to confirm each other and to keep
other readings at arm's length. Freud's account, aided
by those of selected predecessors, is remarkable for the
range of technical questions, and of formal and expressive elements within the carved figure, on which he
has little or nothing to say. He is almost silent, for
example, on posture, musculature, and facial expression,
and on the unresolved interplay between strongly
marked verticals and diagonals. And Moses is unhorned.
The force of a very powerful conviction is needed to
maintain an exclusion as complete as this.

Gilbert Ryle once asked, in the course of distinguishing reflection, or the disengaged thinking of thoughts,
from other forms of intellectual activity: 'What is
Rodin's *Le Penseur* doing?'[11] It would be foolish to point
out that the question enshrines a category mistake, and
that the only satisfactory answer to it is 'Nothing'. For
Ryle was a scourge of such mistakes where they obfus-
cated things, and could scarcely have been unaware that
Le Penseur has nothing but bronze and trapped air between his bronze ears. Ryle's question memorably con-
denses a variety of philosophical issues, and no one need
feel cheated by it. However, when Freud asks, in effect,
'What is Michelangelo's *Moses* doing, and what will he

do next?', it is not immediately clear that his question is similarly inoffensive. Ryle was not talking about aesthetic experience, but Freud – purportedly, at least – is. His question seems to belong to the same troublesome lineage as 'How many children had Lady Macbeth?' and to have an impatience with art woven into it. Art is one point of entry among innumerable others to the impassioned, motivated, forward-moving inner life of human beings.

Moses does not offer Freud an obviously inviting way in, however. Within Freud's personal mythology, the figure is his stone guest, a gross expression of the father's authority and a terrible ponderous recreation of the paternal interdict that weighs upon all human desire. But whereas in *Don Giovanni* the ultimate horror is that of hearing and seeing the dead father on the move again, coming to wreak a last vengeance, for Freud, standing in San Pietro in Vincoli, facing his own *uom di sasso, uomo bianco*,[12] the equivalent torment is to find the implacable creature seated and still. Let him move, Freud's entire essay urges, and let the beholder's motion espouse the statue's. And if a mighty physical gesture is ruled out, this is not at all because statues cannot and do not do things, but because this particular figure has – by an eleventh-hour impulse of restraint – decided not to. 'The highest mental achievement that is possible in a man' is, under the severest provocation, to remain within the mental sphere. The mentalized Moses is one we can all feel at home with, for his plight resembles ours, and his authority has been stripped of the power to hurt.

What brings all this very close to psychoanalysis, despite Freud's disclaimers, is the dynamic interconnectedness of past, present, and future in the Mosaic inner life. Moses in Freud's account acts or withdraws from action in a present that is produced by a constant hybridization of past and future vistas. The way forward takes him by the route of pained retrospection; the way back takes him through his own visions of the future. Just as Freud's self-interpretations in *The Interpretation of Dreams* are a desirous, future-directed *parcours* made up of the compacted and Mosaicized residues of an intractable personal past, so Moses himself, even in his marble fixity, is a set of temporal scansions and patternings: as he moves forward to his supreme intentional act, he brings with him and remodulates an impassioned personal history. Freud, both as self-interpreter and as interpreter of Moses, offers his reader an optimistic and problem-free – because largely repression-free – version of psychoanalysis. The unconscious appears only in its most docile forms, and apperception, introspection, and self-improvement are all given much more weight than they are in the resolutely interlocutory world of psychoanalytic therapy proper. The temporal dialectic that Freud characterizes in the Moses essay is a schematic, idealized model of the *temps vécu* in which therapy unfolds.

Moses' history is 'personal' only in the sense that it belongs to the suppositional inner life of a person, rather than to the outer life of a collectivity. That history is not, in Freud's account, peculiar to anyone in particular. The legendary status of Moses, and his capacity to enact in grandiose mythical form the prototypical motions of human subjectivity, make him an appropriate vehicle for what we might call the impersonality of personal desire and of the time it inhabits. Moses is the guarantor – for all the idiosyncrasy of finger, beard, and horn with which Michelangelo endows him – of a necessary generality or generalizability in Freud's model of the 'apparatus of the soul'[13] in its passage through time.

I now return to the two 'insignificant details' that I mentioned earlier – the anonymity of Freud's essay for the first ten years of its life and the often second-hand and citational manner of its working out as critical argument. What is being revealed in this refusal to be revealed, this search for aliases and alibis, this seeming wish on the part of an interpreter to leave no trace of his passage at the scene of interpretation? There are of course straightforward and commonsensical answers to both my original questions: Freud published his essay anonymously because he was still, at the time of writing it, seeking to establish the scientific credentials of psychoanalysis, and did not wish to be professionally associated with mere artistic rapture and humanistic speculation; Freud cited previous texts, including the biblical account of the golden calf episode, with such care and at such length because he had a proper respect for scholarship, was conscious that story and statue had both been subjected to detailed scholarly examination, and first glimpsed certain of his own ideas *en filigrane* in the work of earlier commentators.

The defect in answers like these, however, is that they have too little to say about the unmistakable grandeur with which Freud dramatizes the act of interpretation in this essay. Before unveiling his own reading of the statue, he masses together, as we have seen, alternative accounts of its key elements, and provides it with an array of putative pasts and futures. But this is not a celebration of plural reading. By allocating a large portion of his own paper to the wrong solutions of Justi, Knapp, and others, and by paying tribute to their intentional density and fullness, he is making them part of his own plot. Other people's errors are the unstable temporal backcloth out of which, in the fullness of time, his own glorious intentional act emerges. They are the clamorous voices that the voice of true interpretative authority is destined to subdue. Freud's gesture repeats that of Moses, not simply by silencing a turbulent multitude, but by triumphantly reasserting the claims of the mental sphere over those of physical action. On such an act of withdrawal to inwardness psychoanalysis itself was founded. The Freud who shyly anonymized himself when the essay first appeared in *Imago*[14] was already convinced that his new scientific model of the mind in process worked for all times and climes, and across the whole spectrum of human individualities. Not signing the essay was a way of allowing his own theoretical invention to speak with appropriate impersonal force. The Moses essay no more needed a signature than the infinitesimal calculus needed one. The structure that Michelangelo's figure revealed was – like psychoanalysis and like the calculus with which Freud compared it – 'an impartial instrument' (XXI, 36) and a permanent basis for future research.[15]

I spoke at the start of a 'safe' Freudian aesthetic according to which the products of culture could be interpreted and evaluated, and have been collecting examples of the unsafe behaviour that Freud often indulges in as a practical critic. The history of Freud's dealings with art exists in both an official and an unofficial version. Officially, his essays offer us exercises in applied psychoanalysis: artists create specific problems, in individual works or in the overall development of a career, and analysts, exercising their professional skill, then provide equally specific – indeed, tailor-made – solutions. Analysis seizes upon details which allow the interpreter gradually to perceive stable and durable meanings. Analysis explains the work of art, and immobilizes it in the process.

There is nothing alarming about this sudden calling of a halt to the production of artistic meaning: it is part of the happy ending that the official history needs. Freud in his instrumentalizing of literature in *The Interpretation of Dreams*, in his reinvention of Leonardo's childhood, in his reactivation of *Moses*, is not at all laying down his arms in the manner recommended at the start of his Dostoevsky essay. On the contrary, he is wielding them boldly in defence of a new mental science. The work of art – for all Freud's connoisseurship and his undoubted appetite for artistic experience – is granted no higher privilege than that of accrediting psychoanalysis all over again by adding an aura of cultural value and prophetic grandeur to its scientific claims. Like Mephisto, Freud declaims with artful eloquence about a mental workshop that needs no art to impress us: the ingenuity, the wovenness, the temporal cross-stitching that we might be tempted to associate with art are already there in the daily and nightly exercise of human minds as revealed by analysis. To write an essay on Michelangelo's *Moses* is in one sense simply to pay further tribute to a mental mechanism and an explanatory method that would be just as much there, and just as fascinating, if the art work itself had never existed.

Unofficially, the picture is very different. Freud identifies with his artists, and competes with them. He recreates the dialectic of their passions, rediscovers the temporal pulse of their timeless masterpieces, and, in the texture of his own freely speculative writing, continues their work of experiment and invention. When Freud teases out the threads of his own 'Revolutionary Dream', follows the forking paths of Leonardo's lifelong epistemic quest, or separates and re-weaves the strands of Moses' beard, he brings into view a conception of science that is at odds with both the inductive procedures to which he often declared his loyalty and the hypothetico-deductive ones which he often used in practice. Inside that topological beard lay the promise of a science which would not only study the transforming powers of nature, but also harness those powers in its own ingenious transformational labour. Those students of art who come to this future-directed Freud in search of a stable theoretical view and an accompanying 'methodology' are bound to be disappointed. What they will find instead are a set of much less virtuous and useful things: a willingness to take risks, a gift for telling stories and making myths, and an ability to remain enraptured by works of art long after the business of explaining them has run its course. Freud was saying something of importance to criticism at large when he spoke of his *Leonardo* and his *Moses and Monotheism* as 'novels'.

NOTES

1   In the monograph on Leonardo that Freud published in 1910, he had already proclaimed this resistance of art to psychoanalytic explanation. There the secret of art had been part of a deep-buried secret of organic nature: 'We are obliged to look for the source of the tendency to repression and the capacity for sublimation in the organic foundations of character on which the mental structure is only afterwards erected. Since artistic talent and capacity are intimately connected with sublimation we must admit that the nature of the artistic function is also inaccessible to us along psycho-analytic lines' (XI, 136).

2   I am thinking in particular of Ehrenzweig's *The Psychoanalysis of Artistic Vision and Hearing* (London: Routledge and Kegan Paul, 1953) and *The Hidden Order of Art* (London: Weidenfeld and Nicolson, 1967) and of Stokes's collected *Critical Writings*, 3 vols (London: Thames and Hudson, 1978).

3   These lines are quoted from David Luke's translation of *Faust*, Part I (Oxford and New York: Oxford University Press, 1987), 58.

4   The relevant passages have been tracked down and reprinted by Alexander Grinstein in his *Sigmund Freud's Dreams* (New York: International Universities Press, 1980), 92–160.

5   The essential account of the political dimension of *The Interpretation of Dreams* is still the one given by Carl E. Schorske in his *Fin-de-siècle Vienna: Politics and Culture* (Cambridge: Cambridge University Press, 1981). On the Thun dream, see 194–9.

6   The critical literature on Freud's essay, and on the Moses theme within his writings at large, is now vast. Among recent works which may be read with profit, are the

following: Jack J. Spector, *The Aesthetics of Freud* (London: Allen Lane, 1972); Sarah Kofman, *L'Enfance de l'art: une interprétation de l'esthétique freudienne* (Paris: Payot, 1970); Mary Ann Caws, *The Art of Interference* (Oxford: Polity Press, 1989); Michel de Certeau, *Writing Historiography* (New York: Columbia University Press, 1988); Richard Wollheim, 'Freud and the Understanding of Art', in *The Cambridge Companion to Freud*, ed. Jerome Neu (Cambridge: Cambridge University Press, 1991), 249–66.

7   For an incisive overview of Morelli's career and writings, see Richard Wollheim's 'Giovanni Morelli and the Origins of Scientific Connoisseurship', in *On Art and the Mind* (London: Allen Lane, 1973), 177–201.

8   W. K. Wimsatt and Monroe C. Beardsley, 'The Intentional Fallacy' (1946), in W. K. Wimsatt, *The Verbal Icon* (Lexington: University of Kentucky Press, 1967), 2–18.

9   'Here we are fully back in the tradition of 19th-century art-appreciation', E. H. Gombrich has written of Freud's *Moses* essay. Extending this historical perspective, Gombrich goes on to say: 'Michelangelo's statue is approached in the same way in which Winckelmann or Lessing approached the *Laocoön Group* or Goethe the *Last Supper* by Leonardo. The beholder wants to know why Moses sits in exactly this posture, what had gone before, to explain it, and what would follow' ('Freud's Aesthetics', *Encounter*, 26, no. 1 (January 1966), 33).

10   Proust, *A la recherche du temps perdu*, ed. Jean-Yves Tadié (Paris: Gallimard/Bibliothèque de la Pléiade, 1987), I, 153.

11   Gilbert Ryle, 'The Thinking of Thoughts: What is *Le Penseur* Doing?', in *Collected Papers*, vol. 2 (London: Hutchinson, 1971), 480–96 (see also 465–79).

12   In Act II of *Don Giovanni*, Leporello, having met the Commendatore's statue on the threshold of Giovanni's chamber, sings in terror of 'L'uom di sasso . . . l'uomo bianco' ('The stone man . . . the white man').

13   Freud's *seelischer Apparat* and *psychischer Apparat* are both translated as 'psychical apparatus' in the *Standard Edition*. On the loss of 'soul' that this involves, see Bruno Bettelheim, *Freud and Man's Soul* (London: Chatto and Windus/Hogarth Press, 1983).

14   The *Standard Edition* reprints the footnote that was attached to the essay title when it first appeared in *Imago*: 'Although this paper does not, strictly speaking, conform to the conditions under which contributions are accepted for publication in this Journal, the editors have decided to print it, since the author, who is personally known to them, moves in psycho-analytic circles, and since his mode of thought has in point of fact a certain resemblance to the methodology of psycho-analysis' (XIII, 211).

15   In other contexts, it was a matter of great importance to Freud that psychoanalytic ideas should be 'signed' appropriately; one is reminded of the disputes between the followers of Leibniz and Newton on the question of whose signature the 'impartial instrument' of the calculus should bear.

3 Comparison between the Arts:
A Psychoanalytic View

Psychoanalysis studies the plasticity or transformability of desire, and is itself, as a theoretical doctrine, quite remarkably subject to transformation. This situation is potentially confusing, but potentially fruitful also. It is perhaps especially illuminating for those who concern themselves with the migration of meaning between art-forms and with the often obscure structural kinship that exists between works in different media (between literature and painting, say) or between the different elements of a composite medium (opera, ballet, 'performance', say). In the following pages, I shall offer a preliminary sketch of a possible future style of comparative criticism – one that would take psychoanalysis seriously as a Protean science of transformation in the mental sphere and then eagerly turn back to art.

I shall begin with a detail from Tiepolo's *The Finding of Moses* (*c.* 1740), which now hangs in the National Gallery of Scotland in Edinburgh (Plate 1). What I have in mind is the diagonal frieze, in the top right of the canvas, formed by the young pink face of Pharaoh's daughter, the older grey face of the duenna who attends her, and the skull-like mountain crag that completes the sequence (Plate 2). Titian's magnificent *Three Ages of Man*, which hangs nearby in the gallery, suggests one

Plate 1. *The Finding of Moses* by G. B. Tiepolo. (By courtesy of the National Gallery of Scotland.)

Plate 2. Detail from Tiepolo's *The Finding of Moses*: Pharaoh's daughter and her duenna. (By courtesy of the National Gallery of Scotland.)

way in which this detail may be read: Tiepolo, painting some two hundred years after his illustrious Venetian predecessor, has recapitulated the 'three ages' topos, handed it over to the main female actors in his drama, and concentrated it in a single descending band of expressive incident. From youth, to age, to death. From light-suffused flesh, to lined and shadowed flesh, to the mineral shell that lies hidden beneath the skin. The twin summits of the mountain form a chiasmus with the uppermost outline of the older woman's hair. Tiepolo has organized things within the main rightwards movement of his narrative design in such a way that this lesser movement, to the right and down, brings about an energetic transformation of ground into figure. Inert nature is suddenly animated, as it is for Wordsworth in the first book of *The Prelude*:

> . . . a huge Cliff,
> As if with voluntary power instinct,
> Uprear'd its head.

The mountain outcrop, brought to life by the crone's head nearby, becomes a gesturing and grimacing *memento mori*. By an opposite and equally terrible motion, the woman is confirmed in her progress towards death. She is prematurely mineralized.

There is exquisite terror in this detail, but nothing very surprising about it at the level of structure. Tiepolo's painting is behaving as we expect considerable works of art to behave – becoming plural, exploiting its motifs by overdetermining them, striving from flatness to a multifarious play of depths and distances. Pharaoh's daughter is involved in another relationship, and here too Tiepolo's irony is delicately reinforced by his manipulation of space: in her aristocratic aloofness she shrinks away from the flushed infant who, sprawling and bawling beneath her, seems ready to tumble backwards through the picture-plane. The princess occupies the place of greatest tension between infancy and death, and the sumptuousness with which she is painted has a tinge of parody. The already theatricalized and nostalgic costume style of Veronese has been turned into another kind of theatre – one that proclaims the lateness of the hour and glories in a knowing and disabused cult of the past.[1] Tiepolo is an ironist and a master of figurality. Hesitation between figure and ground is part of his stock-in-trade. He extracts substance from his ornaments, and ornament from his substances. What can psychoanalysis tell us about an artist like this that cannot already be satisfactorily articulated in formal and art-historical terms? A good deal, I shall be suggesting in a moment. But first I shall set down rapidly some further examples of the ways in which the transformational machinery of an art work may be exposed to view.

The following are common types of event in the unfolding of a musical argument: accompanying figures seized upon and submitted to thematic development; melodies reduced to their rhythmic bare bones; rhythmic patterns extended and elaborated into melody; coloratura embellishments given independent expressive force, as in the Queen of the Night's arias in *The Magic Flute*. We could remind ourselves too of polyphonic writing – Palestrina's, for example – in which all figures have a ground comprising a wealth of other figures, and in which musical structure temporizes between its horizontal and vertical axes, between forward drive and a timeless lingering over its component layers. If we turn from music to poetry with these examples still in mind, certain familiar textual effects may begin to sound 'like music' without being describable in strictly musical terms. Roman Jakobson spoke memorably of the ways in which the axis of selection can become implicated, and as it were gratuitously actualized, in the axis of combination;[2] this meant, in non-technical language, that poetry in its moment-by-moment elaboration had ways of making the reader scan back and forth through the verbal texture of the work and of supplying him or her with more connections and a richer sense of choice than the plain business of making sense required. Donald Davie, in his *Articulate Energy*, describes how syntax can become a species of rhyme;[3] and this mechanism, in his account, is perfectly compatible with the perspectival role that rhyme proper can have in the construing of a poem's syntax.

Examples could be multiplied, indefinitely, from these and the other arts, of a single underlying event-type in which certain elements within the overall design of a work change their status and their role before our eyes, or upon the inward ear with which musical or verbal sound is made intelligible. I am not talking about the process whereby simple structures are put to work to generate more complex ones or kernel ideas are allowed to germinate, ramify, and interweave. Nor am I referring to the stimulating constraints that are placed upon this elaboration of little into much by such shared structural dispositions as the sonnet, the fugue, or classical variation form. What interests me particularly is the way in which the work of art both maintains and blurs its own hierarchical distinctions, by seeking self-consistency for each of its separate modes or levels and then puncturing this consistency by allowing other modes or levels to interfere. This of course happens so often in those artefacts that we call 'works of art', and so conspicuously, that it has seemed to many commentators to provide art with one of its defining characteristics.

When it comes to understanding what comparison between the arts is and is for, and to imagining what ground rules it might need to observe in order to become coherent and decently remote from dilettantism, these structural shifts and intrications offer a special benefit: they place comparison under the twin signs of dynamism and complexity. There are two obvious ways of thinking comparatively in these border territories. On the one hand, the structural vocabulary and syntax of one art can be put to work upon another; on the other hand, a diplomatic language can be assembled by observing and comparing a wide variety of artistic practices. The latter would be a structural Esperanto of sorts, a lingua franca in which the transactions between, say, poetry and painting, music and drama, or sculpture and narrative could be accurately described and boldly theorized. The second of these options strikes me as much more promising, even if more laborious, than the first. Such an approach avoids the loose metaphorizing of one medium at the hands of another that still bedevils much comparative work of this kind. (I am thinking of the endemic muddle that afflicts discussion of words and music in opera and lieder, and of the enfeebled painterly vocabulary that is still often recycled in the discussion of descriptive prose.) Splendid instances of this diplomatic or transactional critical writing do exist: Carl Dahlhaus's essay on Schoenberg's *Erwartung*, in which the tensions and complementarities between the verbal, motivic, and instrumental dimensions of the work are articulated with compelling clarity and nuance;[4] Michael Fried's *Absorption and Theatricality*, on eighteenth-century French painting;[5] Charles Rosen's pages on opera and spoken drama in *The Classical Style*;[6] and David Scott's *Pictorialist Poetics*, on the manifold interactions between poetry and painting in nineteenth-century France.[7] Dahlhaus's work is particularly instructive in the present context, for it concentrates in close up on the dynamics of a single monodrama, and shows how an appropriately 'diplomatic' critical language can specify the disjunctions and indecisions upon which a given work is built quite as successfully as its zones of harmonious structural embedding.

Until now I have been talking about two separate kinds of transformations: on the one hand, those that may be observed within the individual work and, on the other, those that take place when different arts are brought into alignment and are caught up in each other's signifying field. In both cases the theoretical imagination faces the same challenge. What sort of dynamics, or energetics, or kinaesthetics do we need to account fully for the transformational processes themselves and for the expressive intensity that certain of them achieve? I am not at all sure that we need, or can acquire, a single theory to perform this task. It could be that the most convincing results will always be obtained by a prudent hybridization (or an inspired yoking together) of the technical languages available for each structural level considered alone, and that any master theory of their interplay will sooner rather than later become vacuously self-confirming. With this reservation in mind, I come at last to the possible role of psychoanalysis in comparative discussion of artistic meaning in its various modes. What can this theory – which is in some respects the darling psychodynamic system of the age, at least in the humanities departments of universities in the West – actually *do* when confronted with the signifying welter that even only moderately complex works of art can unleash?

For the student of literature and the other arts, Freud's theory has at least two native dispositions. On the one hand, it is a quest for mental origins, for the first causes by reference to which the individuality of individual minds can be understood and a set of typical life-historical narratives constructed for human beings at large. Working in this register, psychoanalysis has a dourly insistent retrospective tenor. It traces its causal path back from the speech, the dreams, the symptoms, and the behavioural oddities of the subject, under observation in the here and now, to the anterior world of traumatic incident which makes the present structure of the subject intelligible. Back psychoanalysis goes – to the primal scene, the primal phantasy, the primal configurations of libido within the triangular paradigm of the family. From this journey back, scientific knowledge and therapeutic know-how flow. But, on the other hand, Freud studies the transformational texture of minds in action, the interference patterns between unconscious and conscious mental activity, the volatile but at the same time seemingly highly organized fabric of the individual's desires. This second disposition is often at odds with the first. The processes by which energy is transmitted and ideational and affective materials are transformed prove to be so intricately intermeshed, and so elaborate in the causal schemes they imply, that any premature recourse to an originating event, or scene, or psychical lesion can easily seem facile. Those who look to the founding documents of psychoanalysis for guidance on the study of art often find that Freud as a reader of mental text and texture outstrips in hermeneutic skill the neighbouring Freud who was an inveterate excavator of first causes.

Another recurrent tension that is visible throughout the formative decades of the psychoanalytic movement will have a familiar air to scholars of literature, painting, and music. How can passion be described? Can it be described at all if it is removed from the articulatory systems whereby it comes into view? For Freud, the psychoanalytic account of the mind could not be complete without specifying the fundamental propulsive forces that made mental events happen. Much practical analytic work could be done on the separable and recombinable ideas or signifying elements that minds became minds in processing, but it never seemed satisfactory to remain silent about the drives (*Triebe*). Psychoanalysis needed to embrace them not simply because the Darwinian legacy had made them into one of the central scientific preoccupations of the age, but because they were an indispensable aid to empirical observation in the field of psychopathology: in the absence of an energy source and distinguishable energy types, it was not always clear how the contents of the observational field could be differentiated and construed. The unfathomable drives, even in a loose hypothetical configuration, told the scientist what there was to see, and the clinician what there was that needed remedying.

Freud's energy languages and drive theories are astonishingly labile. He speaks of libido, wish, and drive, of instinctual force, pressure, and impulse, of 'cathectic energy' (*Besetzungsenergie*), 'quota of affect', and 'sum of excitation'. Yet how occult these forces remain, even when they seem about to become quantitatively measurable, in comparison with the processes of extension and elaboration that they fuel. When psychoanalysis begins to speak of these processes, it abruptly sheds its air of make-believe and returns to the *terra firma* of discrete, serially arranged events. Its process language is not, of course, automatically exempt from vagueness; but the terms that comprise it – associative sequence or pathway, displacement, conversion, sublimation, transference or secondary revision, dreamwork or working through – all hold out the promise of causal connection between earlier and later mental states.[8] In skilled hands each of them offers help towards an exact delineation of structure. And, when they are in action together, these terms can map the switches that take place between structural levels and pinpoint the connections between mental activities previously partitioned off from each other. Looking back towards his ghostly natural forces from the variegated mental interlace that such forces animate, the psychoanalytic theorist is in a position very similar to that of the formal analyst of a sonata or a sonnet or a carving, who pauses to wonder what it is in him that obscurely stirs and seeks furtherance as his attention spreads across the contours and the inner faceting of his chosen work. What animal instinct or neural current or demiurgic energy? Practitioners of both kinds have difficult judgements to make. If they talk too much about hidden powers, the concreteness and complexity of transformational process will begin to ebb away. If they talk too little about those powers, they will be left with a mere box of tricks to study and many pointless exercises in classification and measurement to perform.

There was a time when Freud was thought of by admirers and detractors alike almost exclusively as a seeker after mental origins, and by his detractors among scholars of art and literature as one whose quest for Oedipal origins in particular equipped him poorly for serious aesthetic discussion. But things are now changing fast. Partly under the impact of Lacan's teaching and partly as an effect of the searching intellectual histories of psychoanalysis that have appeared in recent years, Freud's work has become a series of *mises-en-scène* of the desiring intellect. Even in those central doctrinal areas where a monumental stillness once reigned, Freud's thinking has become restless and multiform. Freud reread in this way is more impressive for his wayward dream analyses, his unfinishable case histories, his anthropological fantasies, and his inventive appropriation of artistic materials, than for his tales of mental origins sought and found. The 'new' Freud is a dramatist, a novelist, a fabulist, and above all, perhaps, a rhetorician. Long before Lacan translated certain of Freud's terms into rhetorical language proper – before *Verdichtung* (condensation) became metaphor and *Verschiebung* (displacement) became metonymy, for example – those terms, it is now frequently claimed, had been behaving rhetorically of their own accord: thinly disguised as a psychophysicist or a hydraulic engineer, Freud had set about isolating the underlying figures and tropes by which desiring minds pursued their headlong course.[9] His 'process language', as I have been calling it, offered, therefore, two quite different benefits: it moved psychoanalytic discussion back towards 'hard' science and towards testable notions of causality; but at the same time it placed an important emphasis on the artful processes of speech itself, by way of which the mental scientist had access to all other modes of connection and transformation within his field of enquiry.

It is at this point that works of art as transformational devices come into productive alignment with Freud's account of mental process. Before turning to my two main examples, I shall enunciate briefly and dogmatically three basic principles and say a few words about each.

1 The psychoanalytic account of mental process is combinable with, and to some extent translatable into, the analytic idiom appropriate to each individual art-form. Psychoanalysis is overwhelmingly concerned with the production and transformation of meaning, and is akin, in its search for economy, flexibility, and exhaustiveness in the handling of its concepts, to numerous other analytic languages, including those that are seemingly best attuned to the workshop conditions of artistic production and to the grain and texture of artistic materials.

2 Psychoanalysis, while recognizing the egotistical force of the individual's desire – or the grain and texture, as one might say, of personal motives and goals – is profoundly interpersonal in its theoretical and observational habits. The analytic dialogue is a transactional and transferential affair. It is part of that larger 'web of interlocution', to use Charles Taylor's versatile phrase, in which and by means of which the individual creates, maintains, and modulates his or her sense of selfhood.[10] Psychoanalysis pays attention, therefore, not simply to expressive gesture 'on stage', but to the offstage presences in relation to which such gestures make sense, and to the invisible and phantomatic relationships that any human utterance tacitly includes and re-edits.

3 The unconscious, which is the offstage presence *par excellence*, the unappeasable spectre at every com-

municative feast, prevents meaning from reaching fullness, completion, closure, consummation. Meaning is to be had in psychoanalysis only intermittently, as a momentary purchase achieved upon a constant interplay of levels, systems, structures, registers, intensities, and investments. Psychoanalysis is a theory of meaning not simply arrived at and grasped, but dawning and expiring, still out of sight or already on the wane. The meaning it studies is impure and unsimple, and resides in speech that is haunted by an unsheddable past, drawn forward into a desired future, and always chequered and partial.

My first example is taken from Mozart and Da Ponte's *Così fan tutte* (1790), in which musical, verbal, and dramatic modes of meaning converge and converse with extraordinary energy and wit.[11] In particular I shall comment on the great climactic duet in which Fiordiligi and Ferrando declare their love: 'Fra gli amplessi'. *Così* is of course directly concerned with what is nowadays known as the 'mediatedness' of desire. Throughout the work Mozart and Da Ponte create a range of teasing ambiguities by their ingenious reliteralizing of theatrical metaphor. 'The comedy is delightful,' sings Don Alfonso as his plotting begins to take effect in Act I; but desire in performance and as performance is almost all we can know of desire in this mental universe. Everywhere passion is simulated, staged, spied upon, and subjected to knowing commentary and discussion. Da Ponte's text supplies a complex geometry of criss-crossing perspectives and a dramatic fabric that is alive with ironic sidelights and reversals.

At the start of the scene in which this duet figures, Fiordiligi is preparing to join her lover Guglielmo at the wars, and to this end dons one of Ferrando's military uniforms. There is nothing strange about a further disguise at this point in a plot where so much of the action has already been conducted *en travesti*. In hiding,

Guglielmo watches Fiordiligi, admires her new resolve, and, being a brash imperceptive fellow, sees no hidden warning in her choice of uniform. Da Ponte's stage directions make it plain that Guglielmo and Alfonso are able to listen and watch from an adjoining room as Fiordiligi gradually yields, and as Ferrando's simulated emotion suddenly begins to sound real in the radiant A major setting of 'Volgi a me pietoso il ciglio'. The web of interlocution here is complex indeed: each onlooker has a distinctive view of the scene that unfolds before him and a separate stake in the outcome of events. The characters upon whom they are spying each undergo a change of heart that is musically and textually highlighted as the scene proceeds. The whole drama changes course here. Moreover, the present stage action is not only elaborately patterned in itself, but eloquently recapitulates earlier events. Among several retrospective references in the score at this point, none is richer in irony that Ferrando's 'Volgi a me', in direct response to which Fiordiligi is lost. Its key and much of its phrasing are those of 'Un' aura amorosa', his song of fidelity in Act I; but the earlier object of his fidelity, Dorabella, is at this very moment being abandoned. The 'reality' of his new love is enforced by a musical reference to an earlier passion that has not been sustained.[12]

This fulcrum scene in the opera as a whole has its own pivotal point:

The vocal phrase in which Fiordiligi finally tells of her new love is completed not by the voice, but wordlessly, by the oboe. Charles Rosen, in the course of his brilliant analysis of the interaction between music and drama in Mozart's operas, comments on this passage from vocal to instrumental song: 'Fiordiligi's answer – her defeat – is the most exquisite of cadences, in which it is no longer the vocal line that carries the dramatic meaning, but the long-drawn-out and finally resolved phrase of the oboe. The classical realization of the cadence as an articulate dramatic event finds its triumph here.'[13] This cadence has another role too in the music drama. Ever since the sisters' melismatic swooning on the word 'amore' in their first duet, Mozart has introduced moments of un-willed and unlegislated rapture into the rational argu-ment of the drama. In the soaring climactic phrases of the trio 'Soave sia il vento' and in the duets that launch each of the centrally placed garden scenes, the characters are heard reaching out – beyond their stratagems, their feigning, and their self-deception – towards a region of clear and intense erotic sensation. Each of these mo-ments also sees verbal fretting and point making cast aside in favour of sustained, self-delighting vocal sound. The whole procession of these moments is now com-pleted and superseded in the rediscovery of instrumental sound that follows Fiordiligi's 'Crudel, hai vinto'. At last, rapture has been fully incorporated into the plot: the wordless cadence looks forward, as well as back, and triggers a rapid sequence of stage events.

In this scene, Mozart and Da Ponte have created an erotically saturated theatrical space, but without for a moment offering us a mere Bacchanalian or pansexual vision of desiring humankind. Erotic relationships are differentiated, held apart, and kept in tension. The pe-culiar virtue of a psychoanalytic approach to this sort of dramatic texture is that it allows the space between re-lationships, and between the different expressive systems that are in play simultaneously, to be surveyed and measured. Discussing the dreamwork, and alluding to Nietzsche, Freud spoke of the continuous 'transvaluation of psychical values' that was to be observed on the inner stage of the dreaming mind (V, 655);[14] but this process was, according to the analysis he had already laid out in *The Interpretation of Dreams*, an extremely well-organized affair. Psychical values changed as ideas or images or verbal signs moved from system to system or from one associative sequence to another. Nothing could be understood of the native logic that the dreamwork possessed until the obdurate separation between these internal organizations – the space between them – had been granted at least as much explanatory weight as the general plasticity and compliance of the mental material. By the time the hearer reaches 'Fra gli amplessi', the associative pathway of Mozart's music has already become a complex self-referring weave, and its forward movement has drawn into itself numerous retrospective loops. For instance, the oboe that completes Fiordiligi's cadential phrase has been prominent in the orchestral writing from the beginning of the Andante section of the Overture, where it appears as a solo instrument, and the sublime exchange between oboe and soprano voice has been prefigured in a series of woodwind dialogues that also begins early on in the Overture.

At a much simpler level, Da Ponte's text has certain of the same characteristics: it quotes itself, refashions its witticisms and word-play, and has all the characters drawing attention to the verbal medium in which their destinies are being played out. Psychoanalysis, as I have already noted, confers privilege not upon any one system, but upon the space between and upon transforming movements across it. It helps us to map the separate articulations of desire that are present in this scene (and in this opera more generally) and to plot the points of convergence, condensation, or cross-over between these articulations as they develop over time. 'Fra gli amplessi' is the story of a gradual convergence between the expressive registers of music and text, but one in which equilibrium is no sooner found than lost again, as instrumental sound reasserts its claims as a vehicle of Eros.

Remembering a further, and central, process notion from the psychoanalytic model, we could say that at this moment the elaborate transferential scenario that Don Alfonso has constructed for the two couples – in which each would undergo an experimentally induced and reversible change of heart – has broken down under pressure from a now fully acknowledged 'real' emotion. This is the scene in which Fiordiligi massively switches *Besetzungsenergie* from baritone to tenor, and in so doing creates a problem for many commentators on the work.

If *Così* is a story of two fine-grained sensibilities seeking each other out, and if 'Fra gli amplessi' is the glorious occasion of their mutual recognition, how can Mozart and Da Ponte ever have contemplated a return to the *status quo ante* in the finale of Act II? This anxiety about the ending of the work found its extreme expression in Joseph Kerman's *Opera as Drama* (1956), where the seeming retreat of the four lovers to their original pairings is described as 'in the last analysis improbable and immoral'.[15] This view not only overlooks the role that temperamental difference may play in the kindling of sexual attraction (a sensitive soprano may yearn for a coarse-grained baritone), but under-represents the ambiguity and the ironic guile of the entire work.[16] The psychoanalytic view of desire in transit and in transformation, but flowing always between organizations rather than from one incandescent singularity to the next, is well placed to preserve these qualities of the music drama. Tension and dissonance between the expressive systems of music and text are essential to this work, for they are the very medium in which differences of affective disposition and erotic intensity are shaped and modulated. Mozartian interlocution is endlessly resourceful: it is alive to social as well as personal meanings, to parodic utterance as well as the plain languages of passion and sentiment, to pretence and performance as well as unaccountable delight. Psychoanalysis – of a suitably flexible and non-coercive kind – is in its turn alive to the strange coexistences that occur in the interlocutory field. It has to take them seriously in order to remain in touch with its own origins as a science of speech and with the exalted ideal of dialogue upon which its own therapeutic practices are based. In due course, psychoanalysis may even help us to understand the enigmatic emotional dialogue that runs through the whole of Mozart's music and that Karl Barth caught perfectly in one of his periodic tributes to the composer: 'his music is not effortlessly accessible. . . . This ever-present lightness possesses something very demanding, disturbing, almost provocative, even in the most radiant, most childlike, most joyful movements.'[17]

The dialectical virtuosity of *Cosi* can be preserved by other than psychoanalytic means, of course. Rosen's account of Mozart opera in *The Classical Style* and Ivan Nagel's in *Autonomy and Mercy* (1988)[18] make only glancing contact with Freudian notions, yet re-stage the dialectic and the textural variety of the stage works in critical writing of compelling energy and nuance. Not even their skill, however, is able to catch the speed and deftness with which operatic meaning is created, dissolved, and reborn in the Mozart–Da Ponte masterpieces. The unconscious beckons at this point; but it would make no psychoanalytic sense to call on the concept in describing meaning that is simply lost or latent for the time being in the development of a complex musical and dramatic argument. Extended musical forms are, after all, arts of memory, ways of regulating the resurgence of past material into the continuous present of a work's unfolding. Such forms also allow the history of an emotion to remain audible even as that emotion seeks a new expressive outlet. They belong, however artfully, to the ordinary temporality of human living. Yet the Freudian unconscious proper does begin to have a special usefulness when past material returns strangely and obliquely to the present musical texture. Or when the argument suddenly skids from one associative pathway to another. Or when remembrance, without warning, gleams out brightly or looms up darkly from within a plot that is tidily working itself out. These are perhaps different incarnations of Barth's 'demanding, disturbing and almost provocative' thing. Meaning is not just making itself heard on cue and according to plan: some portion of it is being actively cancelled, and then, by an unaccountable grace, restored. And always at speed. Psychoanalysis has an eye for such mysteries. Performing the diplomatic role that I outlined earlier, trading between systems with its customary diligence, a psychoanalytic approach takes us forward to the moment when diplomacy breaks down under pressure from an ungovernable *Unheimlichkeit* or an indecipherable joy.

My second example involves, at long last, comparison of the kind that my title promises – between the separate arts of literature and music. However, I have protected myself from the charge of arbitrariness that exercises of this kind often attract by choosing two artists who were contemporaries and who had some knowledge of each other's work: Proust and Fauré.[19]

The role of music in *A la recherche du temps perdu* has been much studied, not least by Proust's narrator within the novel itself and by Proust in his correspondence. One of the novel's best-known themes is the peculiar potency – affective and structural – of a musical motif, Vinteuil's *petite phrase*. This melodic fragment seems to encapsulate a spectrum of emotional states and to offer, in its recurrence after long intervals of time, an organizing principle for the narrator's projected literary work. Much attention has been paid by critics to those large-scale structural ideas that are called into play by Proust to prevent the central span of his very long book from collapsing under the weight of its copious descriptive detail. Architecture and music in particular have supplied many weight-bearing components of this kind, and have encouraged critics to 'think big' in their surveys of Proust on music. Two composers are especially favoured as reference points. Proust writes at length about Wagner, and the Wagnerian leitmotiv provides at the very least a useful intuitive image of structure emerging from, or being thrust upon, a relentlessly through-composed literary work. Proust writes sparingly about César Franck, but even if he had said nothing at all about that presidential figure in the musical life of late nineteenth-century France, Franck's 'cyclical form' would have offered a similarly useful analogue for the grandiose repetitions and varied restatements around which much of Proust's plot is constructed.[20]

The problem is that commentators have been so willing to follow Proust's lead in celebrating the overall quasi-musical architecture of the novel that they have often overlooked the extraordinary structural density of the Proust paragraph or paragraph sequence and the quite different musicalizing procedures that such textual 'movements' involve. The case of Fauré is instructive in this respect, although seldom remarked upon. Far from offering a working model for the entire book in the manner of Wagner and Franck, Fauré's compositional technique has been thought relevant to Proust only at the level of the individually eloquent phrases that it manipulates, and a circumstantial question about the composer's role in the novel – 'To what extent did a real Fauré work contribute to the imaginary Vinteuil sonata in which the *petite phrase* is first heard?' – has blocked off potentially more fruitful lines of enquiry. Between the overall pattern of the book and the semantic power of its constituent phrases and sentences, there is of course a multifarious world of textual invention. It is here that Proust displays his day-to-day power of elaboration, and here too, I shall be suggesting, that the comparison with Fauré comes into its own.

The following passage from the closing section of *Du côté de chez Swann* has an 'elaborative' energy altogether characteristic of the novel's textual middle ground. Legrandin has provided the narrator with one verbal portrait of the coast near Balbec, and Swann now draws the same landscape quite differently:

'Je crois bien que je connais Balbec! L'église de Balbec, du XIIe et XIIIe siècle, encore à moitié romane, est peut-être le plus curieux échantillon du gothique normand, et si singulière, on dirait de l'art persan.' Et ces lieux qui jusque-là ne m'avaient semblé être que de la nature immémoriale, restée contemporaine des grands phénomènes géologiques – et tout aussi en dehors de l'histoire humaine que l'Océan ou la Grande Ourse, avec ces sauvages pêcheurs pour qui, pas plus que pour les baleines, il n'y eut de Moyen Âge – ç'avait été un grand charme pour moi de les voir tout d'un coup entrés dans la série des siècles, ayant connu l'époque romane, et de savoir que le trèfle gothique était venu nervurer aussi ces rochers sauvages à l'heure voulue, comme ces plantes frêles mais vivaces qui, quand c'est le printemps, étoilent çà et là la neige des pôles. Et si le gothique apportait à ces lieux et à ces hommes une détermination qui leur manquait, eux aussi lui en conféraient une en retour. J'essayais de me représenter comment ces pêcheurs avaient vécu, le timide et insoupçonné essai de rapports sociaux qu'ils avaient tenté là, pendant le Moyen Âge, ramassés sur un point des côtes d'Enfer, aux pieds des falaises de la mort; et le gothique me semblait plus vivant maintenant que séparé des villes où je l'avais toujours imaginé jusque-là, je pouvais voir comment, dans un cas particulier, sur des rochers sauvages, il avait germé et fleuri en un fin clocher. On me mena voir des reproductions des plus célèbres statues de Balbec – les apôtres moutonnants et camus, la Vierge du porche, et de joie ma respiration s'arrêtait dans ma poitrine quand je pensais que je pourrais les voir se modeler en relief sur le brouillard éternel et salé. Alors, par les soirs orageux et doux de février, le vent – soufflant dans mon cœur, qu'il ne faisait pas trembler moins fort que la cheminée de ma chambre, le projet d'un voyage à Balbec – mêlait en moi le désir de l'architecture gothique avec celui d'une tempête sur la mer.[21]

What had originally, following Legrandin's description, been fantasized as a realm of pure natural process, uplifting in its exhibition of wild, inhuman force, is now revealed as bearing the proud traces of *homo faber*. What had originally belonged to geological time now takes its place in the procession of the centuries and of their changing artistic styles. The broad argument of the passage sets forth a single main contrast – between nature and culture – and then, in a last climactic sentence, resolves it. There, nature and culture are no longer twin contestants in a struggle for dominion over the material world, but 'natural' partners in an endless series of transvaluative exchanges: in the right sort of mind – the narrator's, say – desire can flow freely back and forth between Gothic buildings and the stormy sea.

But the ingenuity and wit of the passage lie in the way this argumentative outcome has already been prefigured in local metaphorical exchanges between the two counterposed themes. The 'cultural' Gothic trefoil colonizes the landscape in the manner of a gradually spreading organism, and becomes a real leaf, a carbon-based, chlorophyll-laden trifolium, in the process. The Gothic style itself hovers above the countryside, seeking its points of attachment, and then, once attached, germinates and flowers. The grand organizing contrast is not really a contrast at all. Art sweeps towards the natural wilderness of the Norman and Breton coasts as yet another untameable natural force.

The Fauré works that I have in mind for comparative purposes are not those that Proust seems especially to have admired – the early songs and piano pieces and the first Violin Sonata, for example – but the late chamber works, which were composed in the years just before and just after Proust's completion of his great novel: the Second Piano Quintet, Op. 115 (1919–21), the Piano Trio, Op. 120 (1922–3), and the String Quartet, Op. 121 (1923–4). These works represent the last blossoming of Fauré's contrapuntal skill, and their counterpoint is the vehicle for a searing and seamless expressivity. Violent contrasts are for the most part avoided, as are perfect cadences and the highlighting of section breaks in sonata movements. Norman Suckling, in his pioneering study of the composer, spoke of Fauré as often presenting 'his successive themes not as a contrast or a balance, but rather as the complement or the extension of each other'.[22] And Robert Orledge has described in the following terms the two main themes (A and B) on which the first movement of the Piano Trio is built:

> Development of A and B in separate paragraphs, either by extension or motivic cross-play, begins immediately after the exposition, and it is always difficult to tell what is theme and what is extension, so continuous is the musical flow. In B, for instance, the repeat of the start on the strings immediately incorporates A_1, which sends the music off in a totally new direction, and Fauré was a past master at fusing apparently incongruous ideas into one continuous thread in his long, organic developments.[23]

What looks like a cult of unity, pursued at the expense of excitement and variety, has prevented these works

from enjoying wide popularity, and certain of their detractors have complained that not only the thematic
building blocks out of which movements are made, but
also the movements themselves, are simply too much
alike. I should prefer to see these works as exercises in
the tantalizing deferral of identity, or in the relocation
of difference from the macro-structural level to that of
textural detail.

What Proust in his extended paragraph movements
and Fauré in his late chamber style have in common,
then, is a liking for near-sameness and for fluent compositional procedures that tend to dissolve the differen-
tial devices – whether of plot or of sonata argument – on
which their chosen medium ordinarily depends. Both are
willing to sabotage a large amount of conventional
sense-making machinery in order to safeguard the continuity of their tightly interwoven associative sequences.
At this point the Freudian account of unconscious mental functioning may again be consulted with profit, although we need to remind ourselves of what is clearly
not the case here. If and when the unconscious is
thought of as having a useful structure-supplying role in
twentieth-century art, the most promising access routes
are often thought to be those of automatic writing,
stream of consciousness, or the 'free' association of ideas
or verbal sounds. Loosen up, let go, be associative, and
the unconscious is yours. Proust and Fauré take a mar-
kedly different route. By way of elaborate technical calculation, they create worlds of pure desire-propelled
transformational activity. Working within the exacting
secondary processes that belong to their chosen craft,
they produce – from afar, as it were – a mimesis or a
working model of the primary process itself. Condensation and displacement are reinvented by consciousness,
and are then allowed to contest or override the 'higher'
structural principles that are still ostensibly in force. The
immediate effect of this upon readers or hearers coming

straight from the products of earlier artistic dispensations
– those of Balzac or Beethoven, for example – is likely
to be that of a sudden uncomfortable de-differentiation
in the mental field. All the landmarks have gone. The
expressive idiom is ever-varying yet ever self-identical.
The concurrent associative chains that these works trace
are presented not as a phased dialogue between clear
and distinct points of view, but more as a perpetual
lattice or tissue of interconnected motifs.

This is 'processiveness' or 'transformationalism' of a
kind which causes no difficulty for psychoanalysis – the
unconscious just is, *ex hypothesi*, a transformative system
that runs on interminably – but which can create real
panic in the sphere of art. How are climax, conclusion,
and closure to be achieved once the dynamo has been
set going? What late-coming alternative principle of
structure can be wrested from the de-differentiated flux
in order to bring its ceaseless expressive striving to a
fitting end? Proust's narrator in the passage I have
quoted ends by talking about desire itself: the motivating
force 'behind' his procession of images and conceits is
at last shown forth, and calls a temporary halt to their
production. Fauré proceeds to the final climax of his
Allegros simply by intensifying and making louder the
seamless contrapuntal exchanges that are the stuff of
such movements. In neither case are we entitled to expect a convincing argumentative resolution or a full re-
lease of tension. The continuum races on, even as a large
conclusive gesture is called upon to silence it.

One safe conclusion that can be drawn from my two
main examples, as discussed here, is that any 'diplomatic' critical idiom derived from psychoanalysis is likely
to be more appropriate to certain comparative exercises
than to others. We could perhaps go further and suggest
that psychoanalysis is of particular use in analysing
works of art that originate in the same broad cultural

context as itself. The crisis of Enlightenment values that echoes throughout Freud's writings is already present in the undecidable contest between rationality and Eros that *Così fan tutte* enacts. More strikingly still, *Le Temps retrouvé* and the second of Fauré's Piano Quintets belong to the same years as *Beyond the Pleasure Principle*, and address the same traumatized European bourgeoisie. Even if we grant the psychoanalytic approach its freedom to travel across the centuries and the continents, it is still subject to an important restriction: it illuminates works that have elaborate internal faceting and high levels of transformative and transvaluative activity, and has correspondingly little to say about countless admirable works that do not possess these qualities. It is tempting to forestall further discussion by concluding that psychoanalysis in its entirety is simply a rather recondite form of Romantic irony, and that Freud will always be at his best in the company of his fellow ironists.

The case of Tiepolo, with which I began, is instructive in this respect. When Lacan came to choose an emblematic painting, one that was somehow 'about' the origins of modern subjectivity, he chose *The Ambassadors* by the younger Holbein, and reread its ingenious allegory of knowledge from the viewpoint of the *memento mori*, the anamorphic skull, that hovers over the geometrically patterned pavement at the foot of the painting. Tiepolo's *The Finding of Moses* is, for psychoanalysis if not for art history, the same sort of work – one in which the intimate life of the conflicting human drives is opened up to public display. In Tiepolo's painting the lively disorganized limbs of the newly discovered infant are already framed by an overarching intimation of death. Eros and Thanatos have been driven into confrontation, and psychoanalysis is ready armed to explore the space of their conflict.

Even when the limitations of the psychoanalytic approach have been fully rehearsed, however, one of its main virtues remains undimmed: it provides an exacting way of describing or redescribing the interactive components of works of art and of opening up new channels of communication between art-forms. Moreover, it can occasionally do this in a way that preserves an important tension between questions of structure and questions of emotional response. In due course we may possess a general 'systems theory' appropriate to artistic experience; but until that day arrives, psychoanalysis will have many useful tasks to perform in the realm of comparative criticism.

NOTES

1 The critical literature on this painting is small, and now dominated by Michael Levey's brilliant pages in *Giambattista Tiepolo: His Life and Art* (New Haven and London: Yale University Press, 1986), 77–81. Details of the Veronese *Finding of Moses*, now in Dresden, that is likely to have been a source for Tiepolo's work, are to be found in Hugh Brigstocke's catalogue *Italian and Spanish Paintings in the National Gallery of Scotland* (Edinburgh: National Gallery of Scotland, 1978), 142–5. All five of Veronese's versions of the subject are illustrated in *L'Opera completa del Veronese*, ed. Remigio Marini and Guido Piovene (Milan: Rizzoli, 1968), 119. In none of them is there any equivalent to Tiepolo's frieze.
2 Roman Jakobson, *Language in Literature*, ed. Krystyna Pomorska and Stephen Rudy (Cambridge, Mass., and London: Harvard University Press, 1987), 71.
3 Donald Davie, *Articulate Energy. An Inquiry into the Syntax of English Poetry* (London: Routledge and Kegan Paul, 1955), 91.
4 Carl Dahlhaus, 'Expressive Principle and Orchestral Polyphony in Schoenberg's *Erwartung*', in *Schoenberg and the New Music*, trans. Derrick Puffett and Alfred Clayton (Cambridge: Cambridge University Press, 1987), 149–55.

Among outstanding recent contributions to the comparative study of literature and music are Nicolas Ruwet's *Langage, musique, poésie* (Paris: Seuil, 1972), Steven Paul Scher's collection *Music and Text. Critical Inquiries* (Cambridge: Cambridge University Press, 1992), which contains essays by John Neubauer, Paul Alpers, Marshall Brown, Anthony Newcomb, and Lawrence Kramer, among others, and the works mentioned in no. 11 below.

5 Michael Fried, *Absorption and Theatricality. Painting and the Beholder in the Age of Diderot* (Chicago and London: University of Chicago Press, 1980).

6 Charles Rosen, *The Classical Style. Haydn, Mozart, Beethoven* (London: Faber and Faber, 1971), 288–325.

7 David Scott, *Pictorialist Poetics. Poetry and the Visual Arts in Nineteenth-Century France* (Cambridge: Cambridge University Press, 1988).

8 Freud's technical languages are studied in great detail, both historically and in terms of their divergent semantic fields, by J. Laplanche and J.-B. Pontalis in their *The Language of Psycho-Analysis*, trans. Donald Nicholson-Smith (London: Hogarth Press and Institute of Psycho-Analysis, 1973).

9 For Lacan's transposition of Freud's *condensation* and *displacement* into rhetorical terms, see *Écrits* (Paris: Seuil, 1966), 511ff. (160ff. in Alan Sheridan's translation *Écrits. A Selection* (London and New York: Tavistock Publications/Norton, 1977)).

10 See Charles Taylor, *Sources of the Self. The Making of the Modern Identity* (Cambridge, Mass., and London: Harvard University Press, 1989), 36ff. and 525 n. 12.

11 On the theoretical background to this convergence and on the new status of music in the late eighteenth century, see John Neubauer, *The Emancipation of Music from Language. Departure from Mimesis in Eighteenth-Century Aesthetics* (New Haven and London: Yale University Press, 1986), and Marian Hobson, *The Object of Art. The Theory of Illusion in Eighteenth-Century France* (Cambridge: Cambridge University Press, 1982).

12 On the self-referential components of Mozart's score, see Daniel Heartz's 'Citation, Reference and Recall in *Cosi*

fan tutte', in *Mozart's Operas* (Berkeley: University of California Press, 1990), 229–53, and, with special reference to 'Fra gli amplessi', Andrew Steptoe's *The Mozart–Da Ponte Operas. The Cultural and Musical Background to 'Le Nozze di Figaro', 'Don Giovanni', and 'Così fan tutte'* (Oxford: Clarendon Press, 1988), 236–42.

13   Rosen, *Classical Style*, 316.

14   My reference is to the short work *On Dreams* (1901) as it appears in the *Standard Edition of the Complete Psychological Works*, ed. James Strachey, 24 vols (London: Hogarth Press and Institute of Psycho-Analysis, 1953–74).

15   Joseph Kerman, *Opera as Drama* (New York: Alfred A. Knopf, 1956), 116.

16   Andrew Steptoe concludes his discussion of 'Fra gli amplessi' with this timely reminder of the work's ambiguity: 'Yet the final enigma is unresolved. Ferrando may be expressing a true passion in the "larghetto", addressing Fiordiligi with genuine ardour. Alternatively, he may be treacherously raising his attack on to a new level of emotional duplicity, spurred on by his own humiliation at the hands of Dorabella . . . In either case, the structure of the musical score, and the grand tonal design linking the diverse episodes of the story, have a transcendent dramatic relevance to *Così fan tutte*' (*Mozart–Da Ponte Operas*, 242).

17   Karl Barth, *Wolfgang Amadeus Mozart*, trans. Clarence K. Pratt (Grand Rapids, Mich.: William B. Eerdmans, 1986), 48.

18   Ivan Nagel, *Autonomy and Mercy. Reflections on Mozart's Operas* (Cambridge, Mass., and London: Harvard University Press, 1991).

19   For a detailed account of their relationship, together with a previously unpublished letter from Proust to Fauré, see Jean-Michel Nectoux, 'Proust et Fauré', *Bulletin de la société des amis de Marcel Proust et des amis de Combray*, no. 21 (1971), 1101–20. Proust also figures in Nectoux's *Gabriel Fauré. A Musical Life*, trans. Roger Nichols (Cambridge: Cambridge University Press, 1991).

20   On the role of music in *A la recherche* there are now a number of excellent studies, including John Cocking,

'Proust and Music', in *Proust. Collected Essays on the Writer and his Art* (Cambridge: Cambridge University Press, 1982), 109–29, and Jean-Jacques Nattiez, *Proust as Musician*, trans. Derrick Puffett (Cambridge: Cambridge University Press, 1989). On music as a 'return to the unanalysed' in Proust, see Edward J. Hughes, *Marcel Proust. A Study in the Quality of Awareness* (Cambridge: Cambridge University Press, 1983), 164–70.

21   Proust, *A la recherche du temps perdu*, ed. Jean-Yves Tadié (Paris: Gallimard/Bibliothèque de la Pléiade, 1987), I, 377–8:

"Yes indeed I know Balbec! The church there, built in the twelfth and thirteenth centuries, and still half Romanesque, is perhaps the most curious example to be found of our Norman Gothic, and so singular that one is tempted to describe it as Persian in its inspiration." And that region which, until then, had seemed to me to be nothing else than a part of immemorial nature, that had remained contemporaneous with the great phenomena of geology – and as remote from human history as the Ocean itself or the Great Bear, with its wild race of fishermen for whom no more than for their whales had there been any Middle Ages – it had been a great joy to me to see it suddenly take its place in the order of the centuries, with a stored consciousness of the Romanesque epoch, and to know that the Gothic trefoil had come to diversify those wild rocks too at the appointed time, like those frail but hardy plants which in the Polar regions, when spring returns, scatter their stars about the eternal snows. And if Gothic art brought to those places and people an identification which otherwise they lacked, they too conferred one upon it in return. I tried to picture how those fishermen had lived, the timid and undreamt-of experiment in social relations which they had attempted there, clustered upon a promontory of the shores of Hell, at the foot of the cliffs of death; and Gothic art seemed to me a more living thing now that, detached from the towns in which until then I had always imagined it, I could see how, in a particular instance, upon a reef of savage rocks, it had taken root and grown until it flowered in a tapering spire. I was taken to see reproductions of the most famous of the statues at Balbec – the shaggy, snub-nosed Apostles, the Virgin from the porch – and I could scarcely breathe for joy at the thought that I might myself, one day, see them stand out in relief against the eternal briny fog. Thereafter, on delightful, stormy February nights, the wind – breathing into my heart, which it shook no less violently than the chimney of my bedroom, the project of a visit to Balbec – blended in me the desire for Gothic architecture as well as for a storm upon the sea. (Trans. Moncrieff and Kilmartin (London: Chatto and Windus, 1981), I, 417–8)

22   Norman Suckling, *Fauré* (London: Dent, 1946), 109.
23   Robert Orledge, *Gabriel Fauré* (London: Eulenburg, 1983), 188.

4   Freud and the European Unconscious

For admirers of Freud's achievement as a psychologist, there is likely to be something piquantly absurd about the idea of a 'European unconscious'. The phrase will seem to enshrine a category mistake of the kind that Macaulay ridiculed when he spoke of 'Protestant cookery' and 'Christian horsemanship'. For, as a modeller of the 'psychical apparatus', Freud attended to its transhistorical and supracontinental characteristics, to those mechanisms of mind which came into operation wherever sexuality held sway and wherever the human individual grew towards adulthood under pressure from the family group or from one of its surrogates. As a clinician observing individual minds in action and piecing together individual case histories, Freud attended to each patient's report on his or her family and sexual relationships. Such larger collectivities as class, profession, municipality, nation, religion, or political party could well be sketched in as background or ambience, but they explained very little, and were granted no determining power in the production of neurotic symptoms. 'Europe' was thus doubly irrelevant to Freud's two-level investigation of the mind: if the general principles of mental functioning were at issue, Europe was too small to be worth studying; if, on the other hand, a suffering individual presented himself or herself, Europe was an unfocusable vastness. For the purposes of the new psychoanalytic science, the unconscious could no more be European than Melanesian or Romanesque or anarcho-syndicalist.

Yet, from the viewpoint of cultural history, the modern idea of the unconscious is of course profoundly – incurably, one might say – European. Whether we examine psychoanalysis in the historical perspective outlined by Lancelot Law Whyte in *The Unconscious before Freud* (1962)[1] or re-situate it among the alternative theories of mind with which it competed in its formative years, it is clear that Freud's dramatic reformulation of the idea depended for its impact upon a variety of time-honoured European theoretical issues and procedures. And the Freudian unconscious has become an object of fascinated pursuit for a whole new generation of Freud scholars precisely because it is so variously reconnectable to a given cultural epoch and its ingrained intellectual habits.

The history of the unconscious in late nineteenth- and early twentieth-century Europe is a ramifying tale of scientific originality lost and found, of intellectual legitimacy claimed and disputed. 'How original was Freud?' is still a question of seemingly inexhaustible historical interest. A characteristic sequence of answers and counter-answers might go like this: (1) he was not original, other than as a publicist, because the unconscious had come and gone in European thinking since antiquity and had become positively fashionable during the period of Freud's early maturity; (2) but Freud differed crucially from his predecessors in that he was a thoroughgoing systematist, and promoted the unconscious only in so far as the psychodynamic system of which it was part could explain mental facts; (3) but the very notion of 'system' that Freud resorted to was a commonplace of the new and topical evolutionary biology that he grew up with, and even when he repudiated biological science in favour of a supposedly 'pure' psychology, he was still adhering to a biologically inspired theoretical mode; (4) but in doing this he was exploiting biology for his own purposes, not remaining subservient to it: all spectacular paradigm shifts in the history of science begin with a switching or mixing of metaphors; (5) but this is exactly the problem with Freud: he metaphorized science; (6) but . . . At each stage in this argumentative game as it is nowadays played, Freud's abstract mental models are re-immersed in their native sea of particulars, and his family history, education, and social background – together with his professional relationships, reading habits, and pastimes – are relentlessly trawled and dredged. Can any self-proclaimed universalist ever have been returned with such self-righteousness on the part of his commentators to the local habitat in which he and his ideas were born?

For Freud's 'unconscious' is European, alas. And it belongs not to the continent at large, but to the Austro-Hungarian Empire in its declining years. And not just to the Empire at large, but to the imperial capital during the combined best and worst of times that preceded the First World War. Freud's Vienna, we are often reminded, was the home also of Mahler, Schoenberg, Berg, Webern, Klimt, Kokoschka, Schiele, Loos, Kraus, Schnitzler, Musil, and Wittgenstein. If the mere roll-call of names is insufficiently eloquent, we can easily remind ourselves of what this astonishing array of artists, musicians, writers, and thinkers had in common: a sense of impending cataclysm permeated by an equally powerful sense of creative opportunity. An old order was crumbling, and a bright morning light was flooding into the artistic, scientific, and philosophical laboratories of the city. But late Hapsburg Vienna placed a special burden on these brilliant individuals as they worked: it kept darkness and decay alive even in their most fervently optimistic imaginings, made savage irony into their daily bread, and shadowed their new-found meanings with panic and despair.

Freud's theory of the human mind contained a moral fable for the fallen times in which it first appeared. For psychoanalysis, the mind was a scene of interminable conflict. It was a realm of competing drives, incompatible systems, irreconcilable agencies or dispositions, adjacent territories between which no reliable channels of communication could exist. Freud tirelessly re-imagined this discord and re-dramatized its consequences for civilization. Sometimes his descriptions have a light quotidian touch. 'The ego is not master in its own house,' he wrote in 'A Difficulty in the Path of Psycho-Analysis' (1917),[2] espousing with some relish the voice of a paterfamilias who has begun to hear murmurings from below stairs. But at other times the voice is epic and self-heroizing: from its Virgilian epigraph onwards, *The Interpretation of Dreams* is the autobiography of one who has dared to enter hell and subject his intellectual and moral authority to a series of truly infernal indignities. The evidence of dreams and of neurotic disorders made it necessary to grant the unconscious a mode of action, a logic, and an entelechy of its own, and these threatened to disrupt even the most straightforward-seeming cognitive operations. For the mind, pictured in this way, not only desires more than one thing at a time, not only drives the individual in different directions at once: it is the realm of the incommensurable, a mechanism installed within the human creature for the production of endless dissonances and discrepancies. Freud's multi-systemic 'psychical apparatus' was to some extent the psychological model that Viennese high culture needed in order to understand its own predilection for irony; but there is a sense of extremity about the first main phase of Freud's theorizing, and especially about the books on dreams, slips, and jokes that he wrote between 1899 and 1905, a sense that belongs not just to Vienna but to Kakania, Musil's hyper-ironical dream Austria. If the conscious mind had ambitions to be *kaiserlich und königlich* in its handling of experience, the unconscious exerted upon it a continuous downward suction – towards the low-life world of the human drives, the genital, excremental, and homicidal urges that high-toned 'mind' none the less also harboured. The very first dream to be discussed psychoanalytically in *The Interpretation of Dreams*[3] – the celebrated dream of 'Irma's injection' – dramatizes the clash between high professional calling and abject unconscious desire, and is an allegorical anticipation of much that is to follow later in the work. In this dream, one of Freud's real-life female patients presents bizarre organic symptoms, which are discussed, diagnosed, and treated by a group of four medical men, including Freud himself. Their behaviour brings together incompetence, spurious theorizing, and demented clinical practice. Simple contact with the clinical material turns the good sense and good intentions of the practitioners involved into a black comedy of self-promotion and obfuscation. It is scarcely surprising that this dream should reappear as a leitmotiv later in Freud's book, for here was a potent image of the worst that could befall the public-spirited instigator of a new mental science.

This is not the place to re-examine in detail those features of psychoanalysis that are specific to the Viennese *fin-de-siècle*. What I shall do briefly, in the pages that follow, is look again at one kind of relationship – between Freud and the musicians who were his contemporaries – and suggest two distinct ways in which the Freudian idea of the unconscious, 'European' or not, may illuminate early twentieth-century art. 'Freud and Modern Music' is not a new subject, of course: Theodor Adorno, Hans Keller, and Carl Schorske, among others, have written penetratingly on various aspects of the relationship. But it has lagged far behind comparative discussions of Freud and literature or painting, and figures only sketchily in general accounts of Freud and the Austrian intelligentsia of his time. Music, I shall suggest, can help us to perceive clearly the scope and the limitations of 'the unconscious' as a critical idea and to check its recent slide into imprecise and indulgent usage.

I shall begin with one of the very few moments of contact between music and psychoanalysis to have been recognized as 'official' and instructive by historians of both disciplines: the meeting between Freud and Mahler that took place in Leyden in August 1910. In such stand-ard accounts of this meeting as those given by Ernest Jones and Donald Mitchell, the relationship between the two great men is presented as self-evidently an asymmet-rical one. Mahler had requested an interview with Freud for the purposes of discussing a marital difficulty, and Mahler was the only obvious beneficiary of the occasion: the informal psychoanalysis conducted during a four-hour perambulation through Leyden produced, we are told, positive therapeutic effects. Similarly, it is Mahler's work rather than Freud's that is immediately illuminated by the traumatic childhood memory that reappeared dur-ing their discussion. Jones summarizes the composer's new access of artistic self-knowledge in these terms:

> In the course of the talk Mahler suddenly said that now he understood why his music had always been prevented from achieving the highest rank through the noblest passages, those inspired by the most profound emotions, being spoilt by the intrusion of some commonplace melody. His father, apparently a brutal person, treated his wife very badly, and when Mahler was a young boy there was a specially painful scene between them. It became quite unbearable to the boy, who rushed away from the house. At that moment, however, a hurdy-gurdy in the street was grinding out the popular Vien-nese air 'Ach, du lieber Augustin'. In Mahler's opinion the conjunction of high tragedy and light amusement

was from then on inextricably fixed in his mind, and the one mood inevitably brought the other with it.[4]

And Mitchell describes persuasively the various Mahlerian routes by which 'the vivid contrast between high tragedy and low farce, sublimated, disguised and transfigured though it often was, emerged as a leading artistic principle of his music, a principle almost always ironic in intent and execution'.[5]

Yet, what is striking about the Freud–Mahler encounter, once Freud has been freed from the role of benevolent counsellor and sage, is the parallelism between the two participants and the predicament they share. At one level, of course, Mahler tells Freud what he already knows, and confirms him in the leading psychoanalytic principle which holds that repressed memories of painful childhood experiences, if they are reactivated in the controlled conditions of the analytic dialogue, can relieve or remove neurotic symptoms. But Mahler is at the same time addressing a fellow victim of baseness and banality, one whose theoretical work no less than his case histories is marked by a syncopated rhythm of 'high tragedy and low farce'. Freud's science has its own intrusive hurdy-gurdy music; his clinical practice involved 'grubbing about in human dirt'(V, 470). The unconscious was at one and the same time the 'true psychical reality', the main source of certainty for the new psychology, and an agency that disturbed and contaminated its explanatory procedures; it provided psychology with its essential subject-matter, yet was never fully circumscribable and available for inspection. 'Knowing' the unconscious was a matter of espousing a rhythm of appearance and disappearance in the quest for meaning, of accommodating oneself to an intermittence seemingly inherent in the structure of the human mind.

Let us examine a precise case of 'contamination' in Mahler's music: in the Sixth Symphony (1905), the cowbells which announce an interlude of pastoral rapture amid the trampling march rhythms of the first movement. The 'low'–'high' antithesis serves, as we have just seen, a multitude of expressive purposes for the student of modern Viennese culture. It sets plebeian music against serious music, primitive libidinal impulse against the 'spiritual' striving of the artist, the brutish unconscious against the artful indirections of socialized desire. But in the case of Mahler's suddenly intruding cowbells the distinction works only by refusing to work. They are 'low' in that they are pieces of dairy-farming equipment, 'high' in that they suggest the uplands and uplift; they are gatecrashers in the modern orchestra, yet offer a privileged glimpse of bliss and resolution; the sound they make is inarticulate and monotone, yet it frames a partial reprise of the movement's tenderly soaring second subject. What is still shocking about Mahler's bells – even to a musical age that has heard far stranger special effects from the percussion section of the orchestra – is not their bovine lowness, but their seeming irrelevance to the advancing symphonic argument. They interrupt. They interject another zone of experience – low in one way, high in another – which, for all the delicate allusions to the main thematic material of the movement that this pastoral episode contains, in acoustic terms refuses to blend and merge. They herald a premature bliss, a higher state that has not been attained in musical argument, but dumped gratuitously upon a still emerging symphonic structure.

Faced with a disruptive blatancy of this kind, we could find ourselves tempted to speculate on the unconscious mental processes involved. Commentators have suggested that a fragment of word-play could have been at work: Mahler associated the second subject with his wife Alma, and in the intrusive interlude summons the reader to the green landscape of an *Alm* (Alpine pasture). But, although name magic of this kind figures in the

Mahler–Freud interview as reported by Jones, such connections cast only a feeble Freudian half-light upon the
movement, and understate by far its drama. The crucial
connection with Freud lies in the suddenness and the
unaccountability of the musical event. In the Mahler
symphony, one structure intrudes upon another, seeming to come from another – obscure, irrelevant, discon-
nected – mental region. In due course, this hiatus is to
be overcome, and the emotional hesitation that accom-
panies it is to be further exploited and integrated within
the four-movement span of the symphony; but, early on,
the gap is unbridgeable. For Freud in one of his theoretical moods, the surest sign of the unconscious at work
was to be found exactly in the unforeseeable grinding of
one structural order against another. In the continuous
fabric of experience, a sudden snag appeared. The rea-
sonable-seeming individual, equipped with comprehens-
ible motives and creditable goals, gave evidence – in a
symptom, a slip of the tongue, a word association, or a
metaphor – of other desires that were not reasonable at
all. He or she seemed suddenly to be speaking or behaving from an alien region. And although that region could
be expected in due course to reveal its continuities and
regularities, its first emergence upon the scene was a
scandal. One of Freud's extraordinary achievements as
a writer was to preserve this sense of outrage in defiance
of his own proficiency as a psychoanalytic explainer:
rather than allow an all-purpose discourse of otherness
and unknowability to inform his accounts of mind in
action, he constantly rediscovered otherness in his own
surprise, and wrote of it surprisingly. At the end of *The
Interpretation of Dreams*, Freud reminds his reader that
the ancients had already displayed in their superstitious
respect for dreams an awareness of 'the uncontrolled
and indestructible forces in the human mind', and that
it was the task of the psychoanalyst to retain this awareness for scientific purposes. The proliferating catalogue

of instantaneous unconscious effects that fills the pages of his early psychoanalytic works is his homage to this power, which he himself called 'daemonic'.

The discontinuity between musical worlds that Mahler introduces into the first movement of his Sixth Symphony speaks of a dangerous openness to fluctuating and multiform desire. Desire has rushed ahead of the opportunities for expression that the composer's chosen structure affords. Re-using a grammatical image of which Freud was particularly fond, we could say of the wish-fulfilment taking place in these bars that 'a thought expressed in the optative has been replaced by a representation in the present tense' (V, 647). 'Oh, if only . . .' has been replaced by 'It is'. 'If only I could experience my mountain rapture *now*' has been answered by an irresponsible internal voice saying 'You can'. Yet, although the Mahlerian wish that finds an outlet here cannot be cancelled or withdrawn once it has made its disruptive entry, the musical language to which Mahler still adheres has of course its own controlling tonal conventions, and these keep a tight rein on the extravagance and precociousness of the desiring imagination. Things would be very different if the musical language itself were pressing towards a new openness and a new willingness to collude in the fulfilment of wishes.

The years 1900 to 1911 were the exuberant period not only of Freud's pioneering studies of the unconscious mind and of Mahler's last symphonies and song-cycles, but of Schoenberg's atonalism and the emergence of what came to be known as the Second Viennese School. And it is in the early work of Freud's younger contemporary Schoenberg that the intellectual disarray provoked by psychoanalysis finds an altogether sharper echo and analogue. Where the kinship between Freud and Mahler is based on a common experience of discontinuity in the human passions, Schoenberg's musical practice at this time throws into relief an antithetical quality of mental life: the unthinkable continuum of human thought and the unrelenting propulsive force that passion gives it. Schoenberg's new music, like Freud's new psychology, brought into view a world of unstoppable transformational process. Such process seemed to be a specific character of the human mind; yet the time-honoured anthropocentric or theocentric devices by which it could be humanly organized, explained, and controlled now seemed only fortuitously capable of obtaining a purchase on it. In Schoenberg's case, the encouragingly named 'emancipation of the dissonance' contained a threat of servitude for the artistic imagination: an interminable sprawl of acoustic relationships. In Freud's case, the seemingly autonomous systemic power of the unconscious sometimes turned the scientific, clinical, or literary practitioner into a powerless bystander at a savage and scarcely human scene.

Schoenberg wrote of his own role in the development first of atonalism and then of serialism as that of an artist who was singularly attuned not just to recent developments in the history of Western music, but to the gradual unfolding of a grand natural design. But however willing he was to become the compliant instrument of history or nature – to do in his compositions what someone had to do – his situation in the years 1908–12 had major elements of anxiety and nightmare. The slow dethronement of tonality that could be observed in the works of Wagner, Richard Strauss, and Debussy reached its culmination in a musical sphere in which dissonances were merely 'more remote consonances' and no longer had the effect of interrupting or delaying musical sense: 'The term *emancipation of the dissonance* refers to its comprehensibility, which is considered equivalent to the consonance's comprehensibility. A style based on this premise treats dissonances like consonances and renounces a tonal centre.'[6] This prospect was gratifying in that it placed a superabundance of musical sense before any suitably audacious composer, but discouraging also: works which were at once long and powerfully integrated now became difficult to envisage. The price to be paid for length was a sense of overall structural slackness; the price to be paid for integration was extreme formulaic brevity. The solution that Schoenberg found to this problem must have seemed disappointing to one who thought of himself as an intrepid explorer of the intrinsic laws of musical thought. For his quest for principles on which to build extended musical structures took him beyond music altogether, and into the much less strictly law-bound realm of literature.

His recourse to poetic texts in, say, *Erwartung (Expectation)* (1909) and *Pierrot Lunaire* (1912) was not in itself a new venture. Indeed, the power of literature as a compositional aid had already been forcibly proclaimed in 1905, at an extraordinary double première of late tonal works by Zemlinsky and Schoenberg. The concert featured *Die Seejungfrau (The Mermaid)* and *Pelleas und Melisande,* and in each of these opulent works an imaginative writer had been given a major formal or form-inspiring role. Andersen in Zemlinsky's case and Maeterlinck in Schoenberg's were called upon to supply both an overall dramatic shape for a forty-minute span of musical invention and a series of clearly differentiated episodes or tableaux. Moreover, the warring passions and triangular love drama that each work sets forth could be thought of as a non-musical expedient for achieving a musical end: thanks to these argumentative literary plots, certain of the contrastive and resolution-seeking components of sonata form could be conserved and remotivated by composers whose harmonic explorations proper were taking them in quite different directions. The classical sonata tradition was able to enjoy a shadowy, intermittent afterlife in these tales of long-deferred amorous expiration.

In *Erwartung,* however, the relationship between music and text is altogether more intimate and complex. In this

work, which is often spoken of as the supreme masterpiece of atonal and athematic musical thinking, Schoenberg tirelessly pursues the 'more remote consonances'.
It is a continuous weave of non-repeating and seemingly
limitless contrapuntal argument which nevertheless culminates, in the final bars, in a closural passage of
astonishing power. Charles Rosen has described the passage in these terms:

> This massed chromatic movement at different speeds,
> both up and down and accelerating, is a saturation of
> the musical space in a few short seconds; and in a move-
> ment that gets ever faster, every note in the range of the
> orchestra is played in a kind of *glissando*. The saturation
> of musical space is Schoenberg's substitute for the tonic
> chord of the traditional musical language. The absolute
> consonance is a state of chromatic plenitude.[7]

Yet the pressure within the music towards this final moment of plenitude and saturation does not tell us how,
as hearers, to proceed in an acoustic landscape that has
no landmarks. The text, with its micro-dynamics of fear
and desire, performs this role. In setting the words of
Marie Pappenheim's monodrama, Schoenberg invented
a language of hyper-expressive vocal gesture whose
sharply delineated contours provide a constant stimulus
to the discriminating perception of the work's instrumental counterpoint: textual motifs are transposed into
vocal motifs, and these in their turn alert us to motivic
interconnections in the instrumental writing. It is to
some extent surprising that the Pappenheim text should
act as a selective and perspectival device of this kind, for
it is in itself rough and repetitious, and expressive only
in a gasping, expostulatory vein. And its tapestry of
psychopathic effects – hallucination, prurient jealousy,
homicidal rage – is woven not from a set of original
dramatic or psychological ideas, but from the sexual
small talk that psychoanalysis had helped to make

fashionable in 'advanced' sections of the Viennese bourgeoisie. Yet precisely the low level of the text, its unashamed closeness to hysterical case material, seems to
have acted as a catalyst on Schoenberg during the inspired fortnight in which *Erwartung* was composed. For
here was a text which belonged, or affected to belong,
so completely to the primitive libidinal substratum that
it had to be resculpted and refocused from moment to
moment: its impoverished verbal gestures demanded to
be vocally re-apparelled. *Erwartung* may have been constructed, in Adorno's words, as an instrument for 'the
seismographic registration of traumatic shock',[8] but it
was crucial for each new shock to sound different from
the one before. The work of musical composition is
going on in terrifying self-imposed proximity to the in-
different, undifferentiated flux of desire and impulse,
and proceeds under perpetual threat of dissolution. In
the face of this threat, the composer had to find ways of
securing articulateness and longevity for his ideas. 'In
Erwartung', Schoenberg wrote in a retrospective essay of
around 1930, 'the aim is to represent in *slow motion*
everything that occurs during a single second of max-
imum spiritual excitement, stretching it out to half an
hour.'[9] This sounds like the language of rapture, but
the lesson of such remarks is invariably one of artistic
prudence. The 'single second' of spiritual excitement,
like Rosen's moment of chromatic saturation and plenitude, may promise a single apocalyptic swing of the seismographic needle, but it makes sense only in stretched-out,
time-bound terms. The continuous 'now' of human
desire is a fine thing, a treasure trove, but it does not
make music.

Erwartung is a response to the problem of creating a
long atonal work of high expressive intensity, and to this
end it uses its literary text in a perfectly ambiguous
fashion: Pappenheim's words provide both an enlivening
contact with a savage underworld of feeling and a stimu-

lus to the invention of vocal lines that will serenely and
abstractly float upon the tumult; they are at once a threat
and an inspiration, a zero point of expressivity and a call
to unimaginable intensities of musical utterance. This
knife-edge is the familiar terrain of psychoanalysis. For
Freud, unconscious desire, the daemonic primary stuff
of experience, lay just beneath the text both of the consulting room narrative and of the clinical meta-narrative
that extended and embellished it, and his hermeneutic
performances have an air of delicious Houdinery about
them: the chasm above which this master interpreter
performed his feats of eleventh-hour calculation was that
of mute, blind, intractable, and unsubduable natural
force. It was the world of Schopenhauer's 'Will', as Freud
himself proclaimed in the later stages of his career, but,
he was at pains to assure his reader, discovered by means
of cautious clinical observation and articulated with slow
sobriety in theoretical models. The unconscious exerted
upon its scientist a fascination so dangerous that it was
repeatedly necessary for him to refortify his scientific
resolve. This could be done, on the one hand, by identifying the primary drives and the fundamental modes of
mental functioning – by separating out within the restless, swarming, encompassing world energy the specific
attributes and propensities of human mentality. On the
other hand, it could be done by the application of practical
analytic skill to those productions of the unconscious
that tantalizingly half-revealed themselves in discourse.
The analyst constructed sequential narratives and firm
explanatory schemes from the plastic raw materials of the
patient's speech; he drew lines where none had previously
existed; and the countless local choices that he made as
he worked were all motivated by an implacable drive
towards intelligibility: such error-inducing mechanisms
as condensation, displacement, and overdetermination
were the defining features of unconscious mental process,
and had to be held in check by a strong interpretative

hand. Yet, in neither case could knowledge of the mind be had from the disinterested pursuit of speculative thought alone. The imprudent unconscious had to be frequented and fraternized with, and its seductive power had to be experienced at first hand if this threatening source of our humanity was to be properly – 'scientific-ally' – known.

Living on the knife-edge, suspended over the abyss of desire, Schoenberg invented a new music and Freud a new hermeneutic style. Both seemed reprehensible to the quieter spirits of the age, and recklessly drawn to their own intellectual ruin. However, what still seems strange about both cases is not their willingness to heed the call of primitive instinctual life, or yet their half-will-ingness to collude with the babble and blur that seemed to characterize the unconscious, but their trusting belief that the passage from the brutish to the exalted, from disorderly passion to a higher intimation of sensible and intelligible structure, could and should be rapid and untroubled. Time and again during this 'advanced' age of sexual self-awareness, the unconscious became Woman, just as it had during the heyday of Romantic agony. But whichever woman it now became – the deranged heroine of *Erwartung*, Breuer's Anna O., Freud's Emmy von N., the Salome of Richard Strauss, the Lulu of Berg and Pabst, Klimt's Judith, or any one of the lesser hysterics, houris, and earth spirits who crowd the annals of Euro-pean culture at this time – she was wondrously removed from the complicating life of the social group. An en-chanted access route to the instincts had been discovered, and the path which led from their terrifying domain back to artistic form and epistemic certainty was now short and straight. Desire no longer needed to be individ-ualized in order to be manipulable by scientist or artist, and the desire that individuals unmistakably possessed or were possessed by no longer seemed to acquire its distinctive features – its case-historical specificity –

under pressure from the desire of others. At moments, Schopenhauerian 'Will' could be seen surging upwards from the biosphere to the noosphere, and nowhere colliding with such awkward angularities as money, work, class, the family, or the nation state.

Schoenberg and Freud both saw themselves as deriving a unique advantage from their decision to remain close to the turmoil of primitive mental life. Despite the risks of confusion or of grandiose mythical simplification that this frequentation brought with it, the unconscious was the fountain-head of all creative thinking. Indeed, 'genius', for each of them, lay in an ability to preserve the elemental pulse of human desire in the higher inventions of the mind and to create a sense of structure large enough to overarch the small-scale daily inventiveness that all minds seemed to possess in abundance and to excess. The unconscious was an essential ally in any such quest for a higher pattern nourished, propelled, and made rhythmic by the ordinary passions of mankind. For not only was it incurably desirous, it was the archive where fundamental human experiences, those of the young child, were stored – not as an inert residue, but as a series of indefinitely re-usable templates on the basis of which the overall system of things could be modelled.

Neither Schoenberg nor Freud had any reason to be modest about his creative powers, and it is clear that for each of them the attempt to sketch out a psychology of 'the genius' was in part a practical exercise in self-understanding. Where Schoenberg's account differs most sharply from Freud's is in its passionate and uncompromising espousal of theological language. Ingenious musical structure can be the product of hard cerebral work, but 'it can also be a subconsciously received gift from the Supreme Commander.' There is nothing light-hearted or whimsical about these self-identifications with the divinity, which occur frequently in his theoretical writings and musical projects. His fascination with

Balzac's *Séraphita*, for example, which was never to find full expression in his musical works, although strong traces of it are to be found in *Die Jakobsleiter* (1917–22), reached a culmination of sorts in his essay on 'Composition with Twelve Tones', where Swedenborg's heaven, as mediated by Balzac's novel, is employed as a metaphor for the unity of musical space.[10] Genius works on the grandest imaginable scale: it has its origins in the depths of the human mind, but the realm that it compels the artist to inhabit in his creative strivings is none other than the mind of God. By comparison, Freud's claims for genius are quiet and self-apologetic: there was something 'incomprehensible and irresponsible about it', and it was not one of the subjects on which Freud's otherwise loquacious new science could be expected to have much of note to say. He identified himself with Michelangelo, Leonardo, the pre-Socratics, and the 'divine Plato', but the psychoanalytic critique of religion as the fulfilment of infantile wishes gave him powerful reasons for going no further.

Freud and Schoenberg in their talk of genius were addressing a problem which was ancient and famous, but which nevertheless had a modern, up-to-the-minute force: after the moment of intellectual emancipation, when a new source of structure and meaning had come into view, with sudden clarity, how could its bounties be regulated? Geniuses were those who could see connections where others could not; but, more especially, they were those who could triumph over what to others was an ungovernable superfluity of connections. But the task could never be easy, even for these sovereign figures. For Freud the unconscious was 'inside' the human being, the essential component of each individual's psychical apparatus; but it could as easily be thought of as something external to him or her, for it seemed also to possess an intractable, self-fertilizing quality upon which the conscious wishes and designs of the individual left no imprint. For Schoenberg the emancipated dissonance was a natural resource that echoed upon the inner ear and seemed miraculously attuned to the connection-seeking human mind; yet even the most vigilant and cunning artist could easily be defeated by it. Both men had discovered a force that was at once a friend and an enemy of form, and that belonged, in an unsettled and enigmatic way, not only to the human person, but to the suprapersonal world of nature. There was no position of safety from which this power source could be surveyed and exploited. The best that could be hoped for was a creative technique which allowed the theoretical or musical intelligence to construct for itself an ever-changing inside–outside zone from within which the quest for form could perpetually re-begin.

Mahler and Schoenberg reveal, then, two different, but complementary, kinds of affinity with Freud. During the heroic early years of the century, when the unconscious was being rediscovered by Freud and launched by him on the most eventful phase of its European career, it could be viewed either as an alternative mental order that occasionally broke through into everyday perception and behaviour, and mattered to human beings only when it broke through, or as the underlying condition of all mental acts, operating uninterruptedly and without regard for the individual's declared goals. These two views of the unconscious – the 'instantaneous' and the 'continuous' – are each amply illustrated in Freud's own writings, and each of them holds out a promise to criticism.

I shall take a simple pair of examples from modern painting, and focus for a moment longer upon Woman as the custodian of unconscious desire. If the unconscious is to be thought of as an interruptive energy, producing momentary snags or isolated structural dissonances within the work of art, numerous surrealist canvases may be called in evidence. In Magritte's *Collective*

Invention (1934) or Ernst's *The Robing of the Bride* (1939), the erotic power of the work, its 'uncanny' affective charge, may be localized upon the picture surface. Magritte's mermaid comprises the upper body of a fish grafted upon the lower body of a woman; Ernst's bride dons a robe that is as alive as she herself is, and threatens to turn her into a monstrous bird of prey. The transformations enacted by these artists – from warm into cold, skin into scales, mouth into beak, and so forth – produce their *frissons* economically, by the mere inversion of a received erotic idea. The desires and fears of the spectator are urgently intensified by those sections of the painting where the transformation is articulated and are tranquillized again by other sections – by, say, a featureless stretch of sea or sky.

In Matisse's extended sequence of domestic nudes, on the other hand, the female body is perceived as a repository of linear and coloristic motifs which overspill the confines of the central figure itself: the line of breast or buttock, the colour of hair or belly, may be freely borrowed by, or derived from, other elements of the scene. Window, sofa, rug, or vase recapitulate and inflect the sensual life of the human body in such a way that the entire picture surface is eroticized. Desire flows across the variegations of the scene, and is continuously moulded, fragmented, and reconstituted as it travels.

The idea of the unconscious is productive in cases like these, in that it invites the critic to make connections between the finite array of structural elements spread out upon the canvas and the indefinite array of drives and impulses that those elements activate in the spectator. Instantaneously or continuously, desire emerges and achieves form as we look, and the 'unconscious' is a useful quasi-topographical term for those who wish to recapture some of the drama of this process: it designates the mental place, the overflowing reservoir within the individual, from which the affective states and libidinal motions kindled by works of art ultimately derive. And it reminds us again of what, in the wake of Freud, we can scarcely forget: that desire is not a uniform flow or force or pressure; that it is shaped by repression, fixation, and taboo; and that whatever 'place' desire may occupy within the mind, it has structure. The unconscious in this account is one dramaturgical device among others for the critic wishing to describe the passage from relatively undifferentiated mental process to expressive artistic form, from an already structured 'mind' to the more elaborated structures characteristic of art.

At the level of critical diction, however, matters are less clear. Freud's own technical language, as is now well known, was the product of a daring syncretistic verbal imagination, and it was a triumph of rhetorical ingenuity. Similarly, the underlying mechanisms that he sought to delineate as a basis for his explanations of both normal and pathological mental processes were assembled from a variety of conceptual components; they were schematic and parsimonious despite these varied origins; and they always needed to be made malleable again if they were to handle successfully the shifting complexity of actual clinical cases. Freud as clinician brought a new rhetoric into play, one that spoke not of systems, mechanisms, apparatus, or modes of functioning, but of autobiographical human speech seized on the wing and in the density of its affective life.

But there is a paradox here, and one that has been given less attention than it deserves by those who import technical psychoanalytic notions into the vernacular of criticism. For there is no compelling reason why those who wish to adopt a 'Freudian' approach to modern art should employ Freudian terminology at all, nor why their explorations of desire at work and at play in texts, pictures, and musical compositions should be expected to vindicate any one psychoanalytic paradigm. Simplifying

matters a good deal, we could say that just as psychoanalysis, considered as a practical science working with
the material of speech, needs to stay in touch with the
specificity of its subject-matter, so the psychoanalytic or
psychanalysant critic needs to speak resourcefully, spec-
ifyingly, the language of the art-forms on which he or
she chooses to dwell. If the critic aspires to be a dramatist of desire as manifest in art or a seismographer of the
subterranean mental forces that shape our culture, let
him or her employ, in speaking of the structuring medium in which desire flows, the most nuanced and discriminating of the formal languages available. In the case
of *Erwartung* this will mean in the first instance the
language of harmony and counterpoint; in the case of
Magritte, Ernst, or Matisse, it will mean that of line,
volume, colour, and ornament. And in all cases, the
additional pressures exerted by linguistic and textual
structure upon the production and reception of art works
will also need to be characterized in appropriate terms.
In the course of such critical activity, the language of
psychoanalysis offers clues but not solutions, calls to
action for the interpreter but not interpretations.

Freud's account of the unconscious in its instantaneous intrusions contains a lesson at once inspiring and
cautionary for criticism. His account of the inscrutable
continuum of unconscious mental process contains a
further lesson of the same sort. Throughout his writings,
he constructs theoretical models, and describes their
possible uses. He talks of 'regions' and 'territories' within the mind; but his topography – like his hydraulics, his
archaeology, and his economics – is a conjectural one,
mobile and open to revision. There is no place within
the individual mind from which all artistic meanings
come and to which, under guidance from criticism, they
can all be expected to return. Psychoanalysis is not that
sort of discipline, and criticism cannot expect that sort
of anchorage from it.

If the 'European unconscious' still has an urgent message for criticism today, this message stems perhaps above all from its early twentieth-century Kakanian phase. For if criticism is to make productive use of psychoanalytic notions, it must remember – however little it can expect to emulate them – the passion, gaiety, and transformational power of Freud's theoretical imagination and the cataclysmic conditions in which it went to work. And remember too that for Freud the construction of a persuasive new theory of the human mind brought with it, as a more than incidental benefit, a whole new sense of opportunity for the cultural critic: an empire was falling into brutal disarray, the European monarchies were preparing themselves for their war to end wars, civilization itself was in peril . . . and psychoanalysis was ready armed with a vision of the human psyche that could make a desperate kind of sense out of this discouraging public spectacle. Freud's tales of the unconscious, seen in the company of Robert Musil's *The Man without Qualities* (1930–43) and Italo Svevo's *The Confessions of Zeno* (1923), belong to a long moment of extraordinary richness and exigency in the still to be written history of European irony. These works all chronicle the survival of the fleet-footed ironist amid the collapsing empires, epistemologies, and value systems of Europe. Svevo's novel, it will be remembered, has an impressionistic and heterodox version of psychoanalysis among its themes, but that, of course, is not the remarkable thing about Svevo. The remarkable thing about him, and about his fellow Austro-Hungarians Freud and Musil, is an ability to navigate dextrously in conditions of extreme intellectual and moral uncertainty and to write with a critical intelligence that is at once volatile and firm. Modern critics of the European unconscious facing their own *fin-de-siècle* have every reason to heed these lessons from Kakania, especially as the destruction of the planet foreseen by Zeno at the end of his confessions is now advancing at speed.

Notes

1   Lancelot Law Whyte, *The Unconscious before Freud* (London: Tavistock Publications, 1962).
2   Freud, 'A Difficulty in the Path of Psycho-Analysis' (1917), XVII, 143.
3   Freud, *The Interpretation of Dreams* (1900), IV, 106–20.
4   Ernest Jones, *Sigmund Freud: Life and Work*, vol. II (London: Hogarth Press, 1958), 89.
5   Donald Mitchell, *Gustav Mahler: The Wunderhorn Years* (London: Faber, 1975), 74.
6   Arnold Schoenberg, *Style and Idea* (London: Faber, 1975), 217.
7   Charles Rosen, *Schoenberg* (Glasgow: Fontana–Collins, 1976), 66.
8   Theodor W. Adorno, *The Philosophy of Modern Music* (London: Sheed and Ward, 1973), 42.
9   Schoenberg, *Style and Idea*, 105.
10 Schoenberg, *Style and Idea*, 222–3.

Lacan after the Fall: *An Interview with Malcolm Bowie*

PAYNE In your Modern Masters volume and again here in these lectures, you don't hesitate to take Lacan to task for theoretical and stylistic excesses. This seems to be a significant departure from your earlier writing on him. Is this correcting of Lacan from within a continuation of his correcting of Freud from within, or do you see yourself operating from a position outside Lacanian theory?

BOWIE I have great difficulty with the status of disciple and with the state of mind of discipleship. So much so that I find certain Lacanian enthusiasts and loyalists difficult to engage with. It seems to me that they're creating out of his works an impossible coherence, a grand system, that is then beamed with menaces at other people who may be hesitating on the threshold. Or they bring a workaday dogmatism, born of this intimacy with the System, to a whole range of non-clinical questions. It's not that I'm setting myself up as occupying any kind of morally superior position: it's just that loyalty of that kind makes me uncomfortable. There are, of course, powerful systematic elements in Lacan's thinking, and these should be got right.

It seems to me that the lesson of modern literature – in writers like Proust and Musil, for example – lies in a certain suspension of judgement, and that one shouldn't think of suspending judgement or of having reservations as a way of opting out. Lacan's hesitation, like Proust's and Musil's, is a way of bringing a new kind of exactness into the picture. Being ironic about Lacan is, I think, a Lacanian thing to be, although it may be, as one twists and turns with him, that one finds oneself rejecting quite large swathes of his output. So all I'm saying here is that there's a way of being loyal to Lacan that has to do with adhering to his mobility of mind and to his powers as an ironist, rather than to the dogma that he also sometimes offers.

PAYNE   The myth of Actaeon figures prominently in your book on Freud, Proust, and Lacan; yet you do not emphasize the version that Lacan tells in *The Four Fundamental Concepts of Psychoanalysis*. How do you interpret his use of that myth?

BOWIE   As I understand that version – which is later than the Actaeon passages in 'The Freudian Thing' – he's talking about himself as destined to be an exemplary victim of thoughts that he himself has unleashed. He's re-enacting in his own person one of the destinies that he earlier ascribed to Freud, which is that of giving birth to thoughts that one cannot oneself control, implanting them in the minds of disciples who in their turn, fertilized and energized by those thoughts, can turn upon their originator and obliterate, or alter beyond recognition, their original force. But there is also a more immediate reference, not to Lacan's own following, who did not seem in any danger of attempting to devour him, so much as to the international psychoanalytic community, which was, in his view at least, maintaining a long-drawn-out ostracism towards him. I think this is essentially a self-glamorizing and in the end rather dull use of the myth.

In what I thought of as the superior version of the myth to be found in Proust, there is a genuine sense of indecision, hovering, hesitation, between different destinies for the theoretical subject. There is no spectacular demise for the theorist, no moment of martyrdom, sacrifice, dismemberment. And there's no spectacular triumph for him either. The condition of being a theorist has to do with a stoically accepted uncertainty on a whole range of matters, and the unconscious, according to Lacan, can be approached only in a spirit of neutrality, a sort of dispassionateness in the face of one's own passions.

PAYNE Does the phrase 'stoically accepted uncertainty' describe your own position and point of view as theorist as well?

BOWIE If only it did . . . But 'theory' is an education in pleasure too. Some of it, at least. There have been two quite separate promotional exercises on behalf of 'theory' recently. One of them is remarkable for the really rather depressing sobriety that the self-appointed theorist brings to literary study, saying 'You've been having an unreflected-upon and uncriticized good time, colleagues, in approaching literature, and we're now going to introduce some intellectual backbone, and a sense of civic responsibility or theoretical rectitude, into your way of doing things.' The other has been a sort of easy come, easy go punning and word-spinning manner. Derrida and Lacan both have this in different ways and at different levels of complexity. But in the hands of imitators, rather than in the hands of those really rather accomplished punsters, this manner quickly gets to be stultifying: its ludicity becomes a sort of verbal and textual tic, rather than a movement in the direction of new ideas. And 'theory' – in the sense of a coherently interrelated and testable set of abstract propositions – goes out of the window.

What I'm trying to do in a small way for myself is to create a fully engaged and theoretically self-aware playfulness of response to literature, which means teasing out a whole range of incompatible possibilities, speculatively, conjecturally, and not being intimidated by the injunction that seems to say 'Be coherent, have a theory, apply it, get your results, and publish them'. Perhaps I'm talking about what the French are happy to call *théorisation* rather than *théorie*. 'Theorization' is one Gallicism that English really does need – to describe a process of continuous, open-ended speculative activity playing upon the empirical data.

SCHWEIZER Lacan himself plays with the two alternatives you've just described, doesn't he, in his strange adherence to precision and certitude; but at the same time his style seems to suggest that he would like to undermine, or at least to question, that certitude.

BOWIE That's right. It's very difficult for new readers of Lacan to understand how that degree of what looks like dogmatism can possibly be compatible with what looks like free-wheeling verbal fantasy. I think that in order to understand how, for Lacan, the two things were mutually supporting and enhancing, one needs to look at the Lacanian nostalgia for – not nostalgia for, *desire for* (let's be projective and futural about it) – a firmly contoured, intelligible, and – within certain obvious limits – readily transmissible version of his own teaching. He's somebody who thinks that certain aspects of that teaching are so clearly an improvement upon earlier ideas of the same general kind that they must urgently find their most cogent, most schematic, most parsimonious formulation in order to be properly sustainable within the human sciences. And quite a lot of his work with topology and symbolic logic and other formalisms tries to create a new atmosphere of simplicity and transmissibility for psychoanalytic concepts that have become possible, however, only by way of an initiatory self-immersion in the complex play of the signifier. There's no easy route to the kinds of certainty that 'the unconscious structured like a language' promises. The path goes by way of ambiguity; but that doesn't mean that all one sees stretching to the horizon is an indefinite play of signification. Those topological schemata that Lacan produces towards the end of his career speak of a kind of structural firmness, a conceptual coherence, that is, as it were, the entitlement of those who have been through the strait gate of the always ambiguous signifier.

PAYNE Looking back to your books on late nineteenth- and early twentieth-century French poetry, with all the careful attention you give there to the problematics of the self in the poetry of Michaux, Mallarmé, and others, it now seems quite natural that you went from that work into Lacanian studies. Has your work on Lacan in fact grown out of your critical work?

BOWIE I think it's tangling with the same sort of problem . . . I was going to say, raised to a higher power, but I'm not sure that the complexity and the intrication of the Lacanian text are 'higher' than those things as found in Mallarmé. There is something about the late sonnets of Mallarmé, for example, that is more intractable, more baffling, more of an impossibly smooth textual surface upon which the intelligence can scarcely gain a toehold. The points of anchorage to be found in Lacan, the formulae we've been speaking about, the guiding maxims with which to make progress in understanding the whole gist of an argument, do make long stretches of his writing that at first seem very forbidding yield in due course, whereas the formulae perhaps superficially resembling those of Lacan that one finds in Mallarmé are themselves so thoroughly ironized, so perfectly insecure as rafts for navigating this polysemantic sea, that one never quite has the same sense of 'At last, I'm getting places'. It would be wrong to say that Lacan is the toughest late twentieth-century challenge in the Mallarmean lineage. I think there's something about him that is in the end approachable . . . 'pat' even.

SCHWEIZER With what kind of desire does one begin to study Lacan, and what are the expectations that led you to him? What kind of fulfilment has the desire been granted?

BOWIE I think that the simplest of the desires involved is to find things out, to grasp the nettle of a difficult text. But what was especially promising in Lacan's work was a sense that it, like Freud's, could bring an uncanny new meaning to a fallen, post-theological world. Freud's critique of religion in *The Future of an Illusion* and other essays is a colluding critique, in that it is an imaginative re-engagement with the very passions that produce this or that need for certainty within a religious framework. So it's an agnostic work that is quite remarkably attuned to the stuff of religious belief.

I see Lacan, who works with a magisterial triadic distribution of orders – the symbolic, the imaginary, the real – as playing out the same kind of strenuous agnosticism, one which takes upon itself the challenge of coming up with a conceptual framework within which to understand the mechanics of belief and, at the same time, asserts a pressure towards meaning that is entirely immanent in the human world. I think all this had to do with my own sense of fallenness into an agnostic condition that I wasn't at all ashamed of, but wanted to make as intellectually fertile as possible. This no doubt drew me towards Lacan, who seems to me to have brought an unusually exacting intelligence to bear upon these issues.

Towards the end of the Modern Masters volume, I say something about Lacan as the only psychoanalyst who's really in the same league as Freud. He handles all the fundamental questions, rather than simply tinker with the conceptual machinery of psychoanalysis. No cheating, no fudging, no pre-ordained certainty. Although one does run into a problem here with the pre-ordained certainty that Lacan, with all sorts of ironic reservations, ascribes to the work of Freud. He talks the language of fundamentalism at times, in speaking about the revealed truth of uncertainty or heterogeneity or mental self-division as found in *The Interpretation of Dreams*.

PAYNE Lacan's theoretical desire is a desire for the All, is it not? That is, he wants an all-encompassing theory, however ironic, a way of understanding the totality of human experience in a way that has, for poets since the end of the last century, become less and less possible. Have Freud and Lacan served for French poetry and French letters a function that is in any way analogous to what German idealism served for nineteenth-century English poetry, a way of thinking the big subject that poetry might no longer want to or be able to reach?

BOWIE In terms of local historical fact, I think there's very little connection between the French poets writing after surrealism and the psychoanalytic writers who were their contemporaries. There often seems, indeed, to be an antagonism, largely based, when it's not based on simple misreading or unreading of the Freudian texts, on the familiar assumption that psychoanalysis is a philistine form of reductionism, and that the poetic imagination, being so heavily committed in the other direction, has nothing but loss to expect from contact with psychoanalysis. What we have in Lacan is, of course, a theory that reaches out towards poets. Analysts and poets are part of a collaborative textual enterprise; both groups are concerned with the irreducibility, the uncontainability, the unstoppability of signifying process. So there's a kinship, a yet to be recognized kinship, between a certain sort of poetic commitment and a certain sort of theory. Lacan has possibly done more than any other writer to bring about this two-way recognition in France. It's just that I don't see poets coming forth at the moment willing to play that particular game. They would all have read some Lacan at the *lycée* or the university, but that's not the same thing.

Coming back to your very interesting point about Lacan and the All. It seems to me that Lacan has two versions, at least, of the All. One is a thoroughgoing metaphysical version, which says, in the manner very much of Hegelian phenomenology, that by this or that modelling operation performed upon consciousness or upon consciousness extended into its concomitant unconscious we can produce a theory of everything that falls within the human domain. From within this edifice we can then cast glances beyond the human domain, into the ineffable. There is a metaphysical ambition in Lacan that has a strange totalizing ring to it.

But there is another quality altogether in his writing, one which seems not to have been taken proper note of and which I would set against that. Here we all individually are, in what we speak, in what we desire, in what we produce by way of theoretical or artistic statement, spinning ourselves out along a signifying chain. I am using Lacan's own metaphor, but one might think an equally appropriate metaphor to be that of an impossibly thin and threatened promontory over an ocean of unknowing. Here we all frailly are, talking our way through, with no end in sight except death, which is already, by active premonition, present in the very words we speak. Here we all are, the fragile inhabitants of the signifying chain, with intuitions offstage of the All that might in another order of things have been available to us. But with essentially nothing more than this word and the next and the one after that to go on and to live by. There's something very exiguous in this theoretical picture, as well as something grandly inclusive. Lacan quotes with approval André Breton's phrase about the small amount of reality that's available to us at any one time, and his theory can be seen as an account of that 'less-ness'. It has, one might say, a Beckettesque depletedness about it. I'm always glad to remind myself of that aspect of Lacan when he seems too much of an enthusiast for grand encompassing schemes.

PAYNE   William Blake has a single word for these two sides of theory making. His word is *withoutside*, which can, of course, be pronounced a number of different ways: *with*outside, with*out*side, without*side*. Theory with a limiting outline, theory outside a limiting outline, theory with no limiting outline.

BOWIE   Yes, that's wonderful. One of the most absorbing sections of the later work of Lacan has to do with the within-ness/without-ness that are simultaneous but never produce any kind of match. There is a necessary, unavoidable hovering on the threshold; all schemes are suspect that offer a firm inside or a firm outside or a firm set of interfaces or bridges between the two. What he admires in topology is its way of modelling the inside that is outside, the intrapsychical machinery that is always interpsychical too. For Lacan the unconscious is both in and out. It is perfectly other than the other addressed in volitionally controlled utterance, yet at the same time, the whole time, something that exerts force upon such utterance. It's a sort of mobile skein wrapping itself around conscious speech: not to be dissociated from it, yet not to be assimilated to it. And that's the point where the mathematicized abstraction of the late

Lacan seems to come very close to an intuition of the poet's. It's a way of interconnecting in speech one's sense of fallenness with one's sense of opportunity, shall we say.

PAYNE   When Derrida turns to Lacan, he seems to be very careful to distance himself, among other things, from anyone who has had Lacanian clinical experience. You've spoken of Lacan as a theorist and of Lacan in relationship to literature and poetry. What is your understanding or experience of Lacanian therapy? Is there a distinctive psychotherapy that is Lacanian in contrast to Freudian or some other process or technique?

BOWIE   What I take to be the distinguishing mark of a Lacanian therapy is the willingness on the part of the analyst to engage with the rhetorical modes of the analysand's discourse and to expose the 'rhetoricity' of his – the analyst's – own speech. This is instead of using the language of the patient as a way of reconstructing lost infantile scenarios in the light of which analytic constructions or interpretations can be built upon the patient's material, which would be more in the nature of the classic Freudian approach. The Freudian approach takes us on a detour, from the language the patient speaks to the originating structures and then forward to new futures for the patient based upon ways in which those *Ur*-structures can be lived with or accommodated to. The Lacanian approach has very much more to do with staying close to the words and allowing a close interaction between two speeches – the patient's and the therapist's – to take place. It reminds the 'talking cure' that it is all talk.

Malcolm Bowie: *A Selected Bibliography, 1970–1993*

1970

1 'André du Bouchet', *Cambridge Review* (30 January), 83–7.

1971

2 'Paris, City of Words: Aragon's *Le Paysan de Paris*', *Cambridge Review* (28 May), 228–9.

1972

3 Review of *Essais sur l'imagination de la vie* by Michel Mansuy, *French Studies*, 26, 229–30.

1973

4 *Henri Michaux: A Study of his Literary Works* (Oxford: Clarendon Press).
5 Review of *Proceedings of the Comparative Literature Symposium: From Surrealism to the Absurd*, ed. Wolodymyr T. Zyla, *French Studies*, 27, 109–10.

1974

6 'The Twentieth Century (since 1945): A Review of Scholarly Work Published in 1972 and 1973', *The Year's Work in Modern Language Studies*, 36, 203–17.
7 Review of *Symbolism* by Charles Chadwick, *French Studies*, 28, 100.
8 Review of *Marcel Proust, 1871–1922. A Centenary Volume*, ed. Peter Quennell, *French Studies*, 28, 345–6.
9 Review of *Nerval au royaume des archétypes* by Jean Richer, *De 'Sylvie' à 'Aurélia': structure close et structure ouverte* by Léon Cellier, and *Le Destin d'Orphée: étude sur 'El Desdichado' de Nerval* by Jacques Dhaenens, *French Studies*, 28, 339–41.

1975

10 Review of *Gérard de Nerval: Aurélia*, ed. Pierre-Georges Castex, *French Studies*, 29, 101–2.
11 Review of *André Breton* by Mary Ann Caws, *French Studies*, 29, 235–6.
12 Review of *L'Ange et l'automate: variations sur le mythe de l'actrice de Nerval à Proust* by Ross Chambers, *French Studies*, 29, 339.
13 Review of *André Breton: A Bibliography* by Michael Sheringham, *French Studies*, 29, 353.
14 Review of *The New French Poetry*, ed. C. A. Hackett, *French Studies*, 29, 493.
15 Review of *Le Surréalisme et le rêve* by Sarane Alexandrian, *Times Literary Supplement* (19 September), 1039.

1976

16 Review of *Paul Valéry: Charmes ou poèmes*, ed. Charles G. Whiting, *French Studies*, 30, 234–5.

17   Review of *La Crue. Une lecture de Bataille: 'Madame Edwarda'* by Lucette Finas, *French Studies*, 30, 496–7.

18   Review of *Infinite Turbulence (L'Infini turbulent); Face à ce qui se dérobe* by Henri Michaux, *Times Literary Supplement* (15 October), 1309.

1977

19   'Paul Eluard', in Roger Cardinal (ed.), *Sensibility and Creation. Studies in Twentieth-Century French Poetry* (London: Croom Helm), 149–67.

20   Review of *Rue traversière; Le nuage rouge* by Yves Bonnefoy, *Times Literary Supplement* (6 May), 554.

21   Review of *Poems* by René Char, trans. Mary Ann Caws and Jonathan Griffin, and *The Presence of René Char* by Mary Ann Caws, *Times Literary Supplement* (7 October), 1157.

22   Review of *Saint-John Perse* by Roger Little and *Exil* by Saint-John Perse, ed. Roger Little, *Modern Language Review*, 72, 212–3.

1978

23   *Mallarmé and the Art of Being Difficult* (Cambridge: Cambridge University Press).

24   *Proust, Jealousy, Knowledge* [An Inaugural Lecture] (London: Queen Mary College).

25   Review of *Colloque Mallarmé* (Glasgow, November 1973), ed. Carl P. Barbier, *Modern Language Review*, 73, 195–6.

26   Review of *Qu'est-ce que le symbolisme?* by Henri Peyre; *Revue de l'Université de Bruxelles: Le mouvement symboliste en littérature*, *French Studies*, 32, 211–13.

27   Review of *Sémiologies des textes littéraires* by Georges Mounin, *French Studies*, 32, 368.

28   Review of *La Vieillesse d'Alexandre. Essai sur quelques états récents du vers français* by Jacques Roubaud, *Times Literary Supplement* (13 October), 1170.

1979

29 'Jacques Lacan', in John Sturrock (ed.), *Structuralism and Since. From Lévi-Strauss to Derrida* (Oxford: Oxford University Press), 116–53.

30 'Freud in France', *Listener* (26 April), 574–6 (the text of a talk broadcast on BBC Radio 3, 20 April and 19 June, 1979).

31 Review of *Prélude à 'Maldoror'. Vers une poétique de la rupture en France, 1820–1870* by Jean Decottignies, *French Studies*, 33, 217–18.

32 Review of *An Anthology of Modern French Poetry, 1850–1950* and *The Appreciation of Modern French Poetry, 1850–1950* by Peter Broome and Graham Chesters, *French Studies*, 33, 235–6.

33 Review of *Cahiers du XXe siècle, No. 1. Mobiles I: Essais sur la notion de mouvement*, *French Studies*, 33, 484–5.

34 Review of *The History of Sexuality*, I (*Histoire de la sexualité: la volonté de savoir*) by Michel Foucault and *A Lover's Discourse* (*Fragments d'un discours amoureux*) by Roland Barthes, *Listener* (2 August), 155–6.

35 Review of *A Night of Serious Drinking* (*La Grande Beuverie*) by René Daumal, *Listener* (22 November), 712–13.

1980

36 'Lacan: An Introduction', *Bulletin of the British Psycho-Analytical Society*, 11, 1–29 (a reprint, with new material, of 29).

37 Review of *Bernard-Lazare: Antisemitism and the Problem of Jewish Identity in Late Nineteenth-Century France* by Nelly Wilson, *French Studies*, 34, 91–2.

38 Review of *The King of Romance. A Portrait of Alexandre Dumas* by F. W. J. Hemmings and *Looking for Laforgue. An Informal Biography* by David Arkell, *Listener* (28 February), 284–6.

39   Review of *Flaubert and an English Governess: The Quest for Juliet Herbert* by Hermia Oliver *Listener* (9 October), 478.

1981

40   (Ed. with preface), *Imagination and Language. Collected Essays on Constant, Baudelaire, Nerval and Flaubert* by Alison Fairlie (Cambridge: Cambridge University Press).
41   'Modern Literary Theory: Its Place in Teaching', *Times Literary Supplement* (6 February), 136.
42   Review of *Comparative Criticism. A Yearbook*, vol. 2, ed. Elinor Shaffer, *French Studies*, 35, 490–1.
43   Review of *Henri Michaux* by Peter Broome and *Au pays de la Magie* by Henri Michaux, ed. Peter Broome, *Modern Language Review*, 76, 480–1.
44   Review of *Remembrance of Things Past* by Marcel Proust, trans. C. K. Scott Moncrieff and Terence Kilmartin, *Listener* (5 March), 315–16.

1982

45   (Ed.), *Cambridge Studies in French* (Cambridge: Cambridge University Press, 1982–   ) (40 vols to date).
46   (Ed. with Alison Fairlie and Alison Finch), *Baudelaire, Mallarmé, Valéry: New Essays in Honour of Lloyd Austin* (Cambridge: Cambridge University Press).
47   'The Question of *Un Coup de dés*', in 46, 142–50.
48   Review of *Balzac: La Cousine Bette* by David Bellos, *Camus: 'L'Étranger' and 'La Chute'* by Rosemarie Jones, and *Queneau: Zazie dans le métro* by W. D. Redfern, *Modern Language Review*, 78, 461.
49   Review of *Camus: A Critical Study of his Life and Works* by Patrick McCarthy and *The Outsider* by Albert Camus, trans. Joseph Laredo, *Guardian* (6 May), 8.
50   Review of *Figures of Reality* by Roger Cardinal, *Times Literary Supplement* (25 June), 696.

51 Review of *Love, Death and Money in the Pays d'Oc* by Emmanuel Le Roy Ladurie, *Guardian* (2 December), 19.

1983

52 'Freud's Dreams of Knowledge', *Paragraph*, 2, 53–87.
53 'Jacques Lacan', in *Colliers Encyclopedia* (new edition), L, 238.
54 'Literature and Psychology', in Rom Harré and Roger Lamb (eds), *The Encyclopedic Dictionary of Psychology* (Oxford: Blackwell), 355–6.
55 Review of *Baudelaire the Damned* by F. W. J. Hemmings and *Les Fleurs du Mal* by Baudelaire, trans. Richard Howard, *Guardian* (13 January), 16.

1984

56 'Lacan and Literature', *Romance Studies*, 5, 1–26.
57 Review of *A Mania for Sentences* by D. J. Enright, *The Mirror of Criticism* by Gabriel Josipovici, and *In the Age of Prose: Literary and Philosophical Essays* by Erich Heller, *London Review of Books* (5–18 July), 22–3.
58 Review of *Marcel Proust. A Study in the Quality of Awareness* by Edward J. Hughes, *Selected Letters, 1880–1903* by Marcel Proust, ed. Philip Kolb, and *In Search of Lost Time* by Marcel Proust, trans. James Grieve, *Times Literary Supplement* (17 February), 155–6.
59 Review of *Swann in Love* (Volker Schlöndorff's film), *Times Literary Supplement* (27 April), 466.

1986

60 Introduction (with David Kelley) to D. Kelley and I. Llasera (eds), *French Theory and the Practice of Criticism* (London: Society for French Studies).

1987

61   *Freud, Proust, and Lacan: Theory as Fiction* (Cambridge: Cambridge University Press).
62   Review of *Intimacy* (Michael Almaz's stage adaptation of Sartre's story), *Times Literary Supplement* (3 April), 352.
63   Review of *Manon* (the Covent Garden production) by Massenet, *Times Literary Supplement* (19 June), 662.
64   Review of *The Balcony* (the Royal Shakespeare Company's production) by Jean Genet, *Times Literary Supplement* (31 July), 821.
65   Review of *Deathwatch* and *The Maids* (the Royal Shakespeare Company's productions) by Jean Genet, *Times Literary Supplement* (13–19 November), 1252.

1988

66   *Freud, Proust et Lacan: la théorie comme fiction*, a French translation of 61 by Jean-Michel Rabaté (Paris: Denoël).
67   Review of *Debussy: Letters*, ed. François Lesure and Roger Nichols, *Times Literary Supplement* (1–7 January), 9.
68   Review of *La France: Images of Woman and Ideas of Nation* (a Hayward Gallery exhibition), *Times Literary Supplement* (10–16 February), 140.
69   Review of *La Traviata* (the English National Opera production) by Verdi, *Times Literary Supplement* (7–13 October), 1113.
70   'Mozart's *Così fan tutte*: Eros and Irony', *Royal Opera House Programme Booklet* (March), 21–6.
71   'Proust's Narrative Selves', in George Craig and Margaret McGowan (eds), *Moi qui me voy. The Writer and the Self from Montaigne to Leiris* (Oxford: Clarendon Press), 131–46.
72   'Outre-Manche' (propos sur la psychanalyse recueillis par Bruce Fink), *L'Âne. Le Magazine freudien* (January–March), 10–11.

1990

73 'Genius at Nightfall: Mallarmé's "Quand l'ombre mena-
    ça de la fatale loi . . ." ', in Christopher Prendergast
    (ed.), *Nineteenth-Century French Poetry: Introductions to
    Close Reading* (Cambridge: Cambridge University Press),
    225–42.
74 'A Message from Kakania: Freud, Music, Criticism', in
    Judy Davis and P. J. Collier (eds), *Modernism and the
    European Unconscious* (Oxford: Polity Press), 3–17.
75 Review of *Pelléas et Mélisande* (the English National
    Opera production), *Times Literary Supplement* (14–20
    December), 1351.

1991

76 *Lacan*, Fontana Modern Masters, ed. Frank Kermode
    (London and Glasgow: Fontana; Cambridge, Mass.:
    Harvard University Press).
77 'Mérimée and Bizet: The Adventures of a Myth', *Royal
    Opera House Programme Booklet* (April), 25–31.
78 Review of *The Miser* (the National Theatre production of
    Molière's *L'Avare*), *Times Literary Supplement* (17 May), 16.
79 Review of *Musical Elaborations* by Edward Said, *Times
    Literary Supplement* (29 November), 8.
80 Review of *Valmont* (Milos Forman's film), *Times Literary
    Supplement* (29 November), 21.

1992

81 *Freud, Proust e Lacan. La teoria come finzione*, an Italian
    translation of 61 by Mario Spinella (Bari: Edizioni Dedalo).
82 'Les Études françaises dans les universités britanniques:
    une esquisse', *Littérature*, no. 87, 77–87.
83 'Bisexuality' and 'Theory', in Elizabeth Wright (ed.),
    Feminism and Psychoanalysis: A Critical Dictionary (Ox-
    ford: Blackwell, 1992), 26–31 and 428–31.

1993

84 Review of *Venice Desired* by Tony Tanner, *Watermark* by
Joseph Brodsky, and *Paris and the Nineteenth Century* by
Christopher Prendergast, *Times Literary Supplement* (30
April), 12–13.

85 'Mallarmé and Lacan: Theory as Word-Play', special
number of *Dalhousie French Studies*, ed. Steven Winspur,
on *Mallarmé the Theorist*.

86 'Comparison between the Arts: A Psychoanalytic View',
Comparative Criticism, 15.

87 'Freud in the Future', *Raritan*, 13, no. 1.

Index